THE HOBBYIST'S GUIDE TO DATING

Sharon Mason

To Vanessa
Thanks for always being there
All my love

Sharon
x

For Rudi

ABOUT THE AUTHOR

Sharon Mason is a TV Studio Manager and Technician for a London University. She has worked in the television industry for the whole of her career, and in her down time, enjoys comedy writing.

Her first novel 'Singularity!' earned her absolutely nothing, but a literary agent, and some stunning reviews from some ex-BBC comedy producers. Her recent screenplay 'The Island of Lost Boyfriends' gained interest from a Hollywood agent, but several painful (Americanised) rewrites later, he still wasn't buying.

Her previous online dating blog got some great comments from friends saying 'For God's sake, you should be making some money out of this stuff!' Hence the production of this book.

She has written a couple of romantic comedy novels, some short film scripts, a feature length screenplay and some really bad comic poetry – all currently unpublished, but she is working on it.

She is also currently working on a comedy drama based on her experiences, and also a dark comedy novel about the Grim Reaper, called 'Thorn in My Scythe,' (not based on her experiences) of which the first three chapters are included at the end of this book.

She absolutely hated English and essay writing at school, but became interested in comedy writing at around age 17, after a Physics classmate lent her a copy of Douglas Adams' 'Hitchhiker's Guide to the Galaxy' and she hasn't been able to stop writing since.

Her other interests include cooking, painting, photography, paranormal research, ancient civilisations, travel, and doing far too much online shopping.

She is 43, lives in Buckinghamshire with her dog and a lot of crap that she bought on eBay. She enjoys long, romantic walks with Benedict Cumberbatch (in her dreams) and hates celery.

INTRODUCTION

Some people say to me 'Sharon, you're always going on dates - every time a different man! Why can't you just settle with one?' (Actually, this is mostly just my mother) And so I say 'Everyone's got to have a hobby.'

Seriously though, if only just for a moment, for this is meant to be a comedy experience, I try not to make a hobby out of dating, although to some it may seem that way. I am, like so many other single women of a certain age, searching for my Mr Right (and a comfy pair of pyjamas.)

It is a quest fraught with danger, disappointment, perversion and general random weirdness (and that's not just the pyjama search!)   It is not something we singletons really choose, but something that is thrust upon us by expectation. The expectations of ourselves, our families, society and our happily married friends, that we will someday meet the man of our dreams and settle down in to domestic 'bliss', or the fabled 'Happily Ever After.' (Although speaking to some of my married friends, this is clearly not the case, so I don't really know why I've wasted the last 20 years worrying about it!)

For some of us, though, the Happily Ever After scenario is not so easily achievable.

A few years ago, some close friends of mine started asking me to write an online diary blog to chronicle my journey as a forty-something singleton and my experiences of dating the opposite sex over the last 20 or so years. Why? Because they'd heard my stories...terrible, terrible stories - stories that begged to be shared in the way that they believed that only I could tell them. They were real around-the-campfire style anecdotes that I should have been able to dine-out on for years! These stories would make couples glad to be coupled, and single people scared to ever date again. These are true tales of dates so bad, that you will wonder (as I often do) what on earth I did in a former life to deserve the luck I have with men.

It's not like I'm an evil person, not shallow, not selfish, not even high maintenance. I'm thoughtful, and generous and I like making people laugh. Ok, I'm a little overweight, at size 16, but who's perfect? I'm very intelligent and have a good personality, and I don't see how that makes me a moron-magnet.

I have tried every form of dating: introduction agencies, newspaper singles ads, online dating, speed dating, singles events, introductions from friends and relatives... but none of these have ever resulted in a long-term relationship. My main relationships have been with people I worked with, men I got to know over the course of several months or years before I started dating them.

I decided to give dating a miss for most of 2013, put off by the constant disappointments (mostly theirs!) and after having several frightful misadventures, which made me seriously reconsider whether staying single might be the best option.

The stories contained within this book are an edited collection from my journals and previous online blog (including some terrible poetry) and some extra articles written especially for you, dear reader. Every single story contained within is absolutely true and happened exactly as I have chronicled, to the best of my memory. I have, of course, changed the names of all participants, to protect the innocent and even the guilty! I try to offer the benefit of my experience by also giving dating tips and advice and revealing a few dating 'secrets' that I have gleaned. (The calendar dates included beneath the story titles are dates when these were originally written and published for the online diary, where relevant)

As with all in life, there is comedy and there is tragedy, but even the tragic stories I have tried to tell with a comedic edge.

I hope you enjoy the read!

*Warning to readers of a nervous disposition –
this book contains some slightly graphic
descriptions of actions of a sexual nature, a great
deal of really bad language and terms that some
readers may find offensive. For this I apologise
sincerely, no offence intended, but I adamantly
refuse to remove for spoiling the comedy value.

THE PERILS OF DATING

As a woman, which I am (at least I hope I am, because I'm wearing women's underwear) when you reach your early thirties you discover a couple of things...firstly, that many of your friends have become coupled and are starting to have families, and secondly, that all of the nice, available men that you knew, are no longer available (or even that nice.) The social life you had in your twenties with your single friends of both sexes, has suddenly ground to a halt. Your married friends will stop inviting you round for dinner, and will choose instead to only spend time with other marrieds with whom they feel safe. To them, you will become an object of bizarre fascination, much in the same way as The Elephant Man or Keith Lemon.

At this stage, it's quite normal to do one of two things; either you throw yourself into your career, knitting jumpers for bald chickens, scrapbooking (yes, that actually is a thing apparently) and doing charity 'fun' runs. Or, you start to panic-date.

Resigning yourself to 'spinsterhood' might seem like the tough option, but in my opinion the even tougher decision is to start pimping yourself out on the dating scene. When panic mode sets in, you will, against your own better judgement, join as many online dating agencies as you can find, and start going to speed dating events.

Hold tight, because you are about to experience the perils of dating out of your comfort zone. And by 'out of your comfort zone' I mean with complete strangers, or those not within your social circle and mostly probably never likely to be, either. It's a bit like entering The Twilight Zone.

When expectations are not met
We all have high expectations of our dates, but when our date appears not 'as advertised', we can't help but feel cheated.
Prince Charming, once good on paper, in reality can be Lord Voldemort. The beaming smile, shown on his profile photograph, may have just been from a moment of schadenfreude. What I'm saying is, if you're expecting Russell Crowe, just don't be surprised if Russell Brand shows up.

No matter what they've written in their profile, or what photographic proof they have offered, your date will invariably turn out to be either older, balder, shorter, fatter, madder or kinkier than originally suggested. On a dating site, never take anything at face value.

Having to make small talk
Being faced with the reality (you're actually on a date with a hobbit, and not with the heir to the throne of Gondor) you're likely to want to turn and run. But if you are a decent and reasonable person, you will of course give them a chance to make a complete tit of themselves before prejudging them, or asking them if they've already had second breakfast.

You'll start by making small talk. If you're British it is mandatory to include comment on the weather. (I'm not sure what the US equivalent of this is, it may vary state to state, but I should imagine it has something to do with baseball.) Other variants of small talk can include questions regarding their journey, whether they've visited the venue previously and whether they presently have any mild contagions.

But what do you do when someone says to you (and this has happened to me) that they 'don't do small talk'? It's tempting to just launch into something completely over their heads like quantum physics or the nature of the universe, but what if they just mean that they want to just cut to the chase? Never mind the weather...do you want sex with the hobbit or don't you? (They may of course have other names for their genitalia that are not Tolkien related.) Beware of these men, who dislike the 'niceties' of dating - they are either married or are simply perverts – I would avoid them at all cost.

Of course most normal people don't have a problem with a bit of small talk to start off with, and when that's out of the way, you can start with the more probing questions. You'll attempt to fill the silences, as he won't necessarily have thought of anything to ask you. So you will start to sound a bit like a mad inquisitor. Beads of sweat will start to form on his forehead. What do you do for work? What do you like doing in your spare time? Have you travelled much out of the Shire? What do you think of Coldplay?

The dreaded 'will we? won't we?'
During the first five minutes of the date you will have made a decision about whether you want to see this person again. More often than not, you will decide that you would rather die single with a house full of cats, than to spend another minute in the company of this individual. But occasionally (very very rarely) you will have had a reasonably pleasant date and will want to see the person again.

When do you bring up the question of a second date? If you don't like them, wait and see if they ask you. If they do ask, be vague. Don't make any promises you can't keep. Tell them you'll arrange something by text and then message them later with 'Sorry but I didn't think there was any chemistry.'

If you do really want to see them again and they haven't asked you, then you could either try asking them, if you're feeling brave, or wait until later and ask them by text. If they say 'Sorry but I didn't think there was any chemistry' then they've probably also been reading this book, and it's their loss. Move on. Do not become obsessed by them and start stalking them on Facebook or making rude comments about them on Twitter.

Making your excuses
If the date is going very badly indeed, you might want to cut your losses and just get out of there. There are several escape methods you can use...

The Emergency – Everyone's used this one at some point...Get a friend to call you mid-date and stage either a plumbing emergency, a family health issue, or similar scenario.

You can arrange this while visiting the toilets, but don't forget to take your phone with you, or this may be slightly more difficult to arrange. (This also works for other socials that you want to ditch.)

The Early Wake-Up. Business meeting? Early flight? Make it up, you can be creative here.

The Can't Stay Late date – exactly what it says on the tin. Establish within the first 5 minutes that it'll be a short date because you've arranged to be somewhere else later.

The Useful Dependants. Use your dependants wisely. You can say you've got to get back for your dog/cat/ child/ sick grandmother, but saying that you forgot to feed your fish might be pushing it a little.

The Off-Putter – tell the date something truly horrendous about yourself (ideally a lie) that will put them off immediately. Something like 'Oh shit! I forgot to tell my husband that I'd be out so late.'

The Fast Forward - try speaking at double speed, it'll shorten the date by half.

Wet yourself and let nature take its course.

The Goodbye – to kiss or not to kiss
At the end of the date, there's always that
awkward moment (I don't mean the one about
who gets the bill) Will he go for a peck on the
cheek, an out-and-out refusal to get close, or a
full on grope? If he is a gentleman, he will
politely kiss you on the cheek and see you to
your car. If he is not a gentleman (they can be
rare these days) he will either disappear into the
night without a backward glance or he will try to
stick his tongue down your throat and his hand
up your top. If this happens, quickly make you
excuses and leave, fast. Do not take him home
for coffee, or any other hot beverage.

The worst part of all – waiting for the call
If you've texted him and told him that you'd like
to meet up again then just wait it out. If he
really wants to see you again then he will make
it happen. If he has not texted you back straight
away then he may just be busy, so don't get
paranoid just yet. Don't update your status on
Facebook prematurely with 'in a relationship'
until you've been dating a good few weeks at
least and it has been mutually agreed.

And if you don't hear from him, then put it down to experience and put yourself out there again as soon as possible. The more practice you have, the better you'll get, and you may even get enough material together to write a book about your terrible dating experiences.

CHEESECAKE MAN

Summer 2004

Matt was gorgeous. Funny, intelligent, great job, great car, great apartment and good taste in home furnishings. How was this man still single? I asked myself. Perhaps an alarm bell should have rung. But it didn't.
Our first date was full of promise. We got on like a house on fire. Intelligent conversation, good food. I made him laugh, he made me laugh, and he didn't seem to have any outward signs of being a fuckwit. And at the end of the first date, a long and passionate kiss, to which he remarked 'I should have left room for dessert.' Ten dates followed over the course of the next 2 weeks! I thought this was it. I'd finally found The One.

But things were getting weird. By the time we'd been on about 7 dates, there still hadn't been another kiss. I was getting desperate. What was going wrong? Luckily, the perfect excuse presented itself for me to stay over at his place (my place was haunted!) and as unfortunately (!) he didn't have a spare bed, I was going to have to share with him. What a shame!

Now, most normal, red-bloodied men would have trouble keeping their hands off a half-naked woman, sleeping in their bed, but not Matt. He was the perfect gentleman (the bastard!) Not even a peck on the cheek. I got up early to use his bathroom, and when I got back to bed I thought something had changed, he draped a hand and leg over me! But still nothing happened.

More dates followed. I was to stay over at his place once more, and experience his cooking. He told me he always kept a tub of mascarpone cheese in the fridge for just in case he wanted to make a cheesecake. Now I was beginning to wonder.

As I lay in his bed, that night, I wondered if there was any chance he was just being a gentleman. So I decided to make my move. I kissed him passionately, but I could tell there was nothing on the other side of the kiss. I asked him why. He said I was like a sister to him! He said he normally dated really beautiful women, and that I wasn't as attractive as them! Bloody cheek!

(And here's the song I dedicated to him - to the tune of Lily Allen's 'It's Not Fair') (Do not read if you are easily offended. No offence to my gay friends is intended here, I love you all!)

Oh we have a lot in common and he loves to make me laugh,

He calls me all the time, he even calls me in the bath,
He's intelligent and kind and just the type that I would seek,
We've been on fourteen dates already, only known him for a week...

But there's one thing that's getting in the way
You have great taste in cushions, and I think you might be gay
I look into your eyes, I want you to be my mister
But then you go and tell me, I kiss just like your sister

It's not fair, I think I'm really keen
I think I'm really keen, Yes I think I'm really keen,
Oh you should be in love, but you're acting like a queen
You're acting like a queen.

I lie here naked in your bedroom as you mince around in shorts
But you never get a hard-on and I'm getting kinda bored
You invite me to sleep over, but it isn't love we make
You've bought a tub of mascarpone and you've rustled up cheesecake.

There's just one thing that's getting in the way

I really like your curtains, I think you might be
gay
I look into your eyes, I think I'm getting wise
and
Now it seems to me, that you're a fan of
Streisand.

It's not fair I think I'm really keen
I think I'm really keen, Yes I think I'm really
keen
Oh you should be in love, but you're acting like
a queen
You're acting like a queen.

You like to watch Rock Hudson, Oh I think it's
kinda lame
How about we spice the evening up? Why don't
we play a little game?
I suggest to you strip poker, but you prefer
Monopoly
Now I think I've got it figured, you're a friend of
Dorothy....

THE HELICOPTER

December 2010

Fred was a guy that I actually asked out. He'd repaired my computer a couple of times and I thought he was quite cute, in a geeky sort of way, and he looked a bit like Justin Long (the actor).

Our first date was full of romantic promise...a walk in the snow, a kiss under some wild mistletoe, and a heated...game of scrabble. So I agreed to a second date, but this was to prove slightly less romantic.

The following evening, he came over for dinner. I cooked, and then asked him if he'd ever seen the greatest movie ever made. He said he hadn't. But as we sat and watched the DVD together, it wasn't 15 minutes in before he got his knob out and started waving it around like a helicopter, hoping I would notice and want to use it as a lollipop!

But the worst was still to come. The ultimate nail in the coffin moment, he said (and I am in no way exaggerating, this is word for word) 'I want to get you pregnant and then I'm going to marry you!'

20

Well, after that, he was out of my life so fast he barely had time to fasten his cycle clips. And the real shame, I shall never be able to watch 'The Shawshank Redemption' again in the same light.

ROMANCE REALLY IS DEAD

In early 2012, I went back to an online dating agency that I haven't used in a while, mostly because they're all full of time-wasters! But I had hoped that maybe, just maybe, this time I might meet someone nice and genuine.

I had a few messages, mostly along the lines of 'You look hot / lush / horny / etc etc' clearly from people with no respect for women, which were deleted immediately. Anyway, I replied to some of the better sounding ones, and lined up a couple of dates.

One of these men, Andy seemed genuine and nice for starters, but then as we started texting about meeting up, I got the impression that he wasn't as nice as I originally thought. With his question 'How busty are you?' I suddenly got that sinking feeling of 'Oh no, not again!'

He then decided that for our first date he wanted to come over to my place for a home cooked 'romantic' meal, and wanted me to 'put him up' for the night, as he didn't live very near. I told him that for a first date that wasn't appropriate, and I suggested meeting for a drink somewhere neutral.

(Clearly it wasn't romance that was on his mind.) By that time I'd decided enough was enough, and wasn't prepared to waste my time any longer.

He then texted to ask me if I wanted children. I said I didn't, but that it said that in my online profile (which if he'd actually read, he'd know that.) He wished me well. I didn't respond. But in my head I wished him a painful STD.

THE LOVE TRAP

Summer 2010

Gerry was another internet date, and I already knew that he and I wouldn't get on even before I met him. Maybe I just do it for the anecdotes! His online profile stated that he enjoyed horror movies, especially 'Saw', and that he wanted to 'trap someone with romance'. He worked in purchase ledger for a well-known Japanese video brand, and when we spoke on the phone, he tried to impress me by telling me that he 'regularly transfers large sums of money between here and Tokyo.' Not sure why he thought that would impress me. If it had been his own money, I might have been more prone to congratulation, but I simply rolled my eyes and prayed to the maker that this be over quickly.

Also on the phone, he told me that he had a list of questions for me. 'Great' I thought, finally someone actually wants to get to know the real me. But I should have known better. 'Fire away,' I said. His first question (no word of a lie) was: 'Have you ever been to Marwell Zoo?'

I was, quite frankly, gobsmacked. What do you say to that? I said 'No,' and wondered why the hell that was relevant. After his second question I realised what he was getting at.

'Have you ever been to Egypt and seen the Pyramids and stuff?' (Stuff????) (I had actually seen the pyramids. I'd seen the 'stuff' too!) I realised that this man was desperate. Desperate to have someone else to go places with. It didn't matter who it was, or what they were like. All that mattered was that he had someone on his arm, some comfort blanket, because he was too scared to go out on his own. The poor, pathetic little lamb. He didn't actually ask anything about me at all.

On the actual date, at a local pub, he turned up with a bottle of champagne (in a wine cooler!) a tub of strawberries, a bouquet of red roses and some rubber balls for my dog. Yes, he screamed desperation. (This was going to be fun.) He expected me to consume the strawberries and champagne at the pub, to which I told him, firstly, that I didn't drink champagne (had he actually asked me anything relevant on the phone, he might have learned that I'm not big on alcohol) and secondly, that you're not allowed to consume your own food and drink at a pub. He ended up taking the champagne home.

During the date I was in a mischievous mood and was determined to be difficult. I'd made absolutely no effort, wore no make-up and was set to disagree with everything he said. He told me he'd just bought a new plasma TV (apparently the best on the market) and so I told him that plasma TVs were awful and the displays were easily damaged. He explained why he liked horror films, and I explained that I thought they were stupid and pointless and that there was enough horror on the news without having it bandied around as entertainment.

I had made myself as disagreeable as possible, but this man was so desperate, he asked me for a second date. I turned him down - I really couldn't see myself being trapped in romance with this person.

SPEED-DATING – AN INTRODUCTION

On occasions (rare occasions)... (OK, desperate occasions) when either my friend, Sue, fancies trying out the dating scene again, or when I run out of pant-wettingly funny anecdotes to tell around the dinner table, we decide to put on our emotional armour, have the taxi on stand-by, and brave the bizarre and completely disappointing world of Speed Dating.
I prefer to call it 'Speed-Friending' as no one ever leaves a speed-dating event with a date. Ever.

All the men in the room only want to date the pretty, skinny, blonde girl, and the pretty skinny, blonde girl couldn't give a toss about the men there because: a) They're mostly freaks, and she's too far out of their leagues to give them the time of day, and b) She's only there to offer moral support to her fat friend.

She could, of course, have her pick of any of the men in there, if only she weren't already dating the captain of the football team / the founder member of MENSA / George Clooney (delete as appropriate.)

The fact that she has the personality of a haddock, will only date 'men who have dogs' (currently living, not deceased) and has to have her beverage served at exactly 4 degrees centigrade, does nothing to quell their ardent admiration for her.   These women are known as 'high-maintenance' and for some strange reason always seem to get the most sought-after men. The reason for this is a complete mystery and will not be answered in this book!   So, enough of the bitterness and back to the main event...

1. **During a speed-dating event, the purpose is to look as if you care what the other person is talking about**...even if they spend the entire 5 minutes talking about oil rigs. This is known as 'acting' and all regular speed-dating 'professionals' will be aware of how to use it to their advantage. You will most likely be wondering whether you should have grabbed a 6-pack portion of Chicken Nuggets on your way there, and hoping that your calls of 'TAXI!' will be heard once you run screaming out into the street.

2. **Smile.** Even if you are faced with an arrogant arsehole of a man who clearly doesn't want to be within 200 miles of you and says he is only there to 'make up the numbers'.

3. **Ask interesting questions.** Do NOT, and I repeat NOT ask whether or not your date-ette has recently been to Marwell Zoo. You may, however, ask about their jobs, their interests, their travels or even what food photographs they've posted on Facebook recently. If they say they are into science, probe further. You may well find out that you actually know more about quantum physics than they do. If an awkward silence follows, revert to point number 2 and ask them whether or not they're ever been to Marwell zoo.

4. **Prepare questions in advance.** The speed-dating host may offer some suggestions as to what sort of questions to ask, for example 'How would your friends describe you?' The answer is most likely to be 'desperate' but you'll have time to think of other more alluring answers, if you prefer.

5. **Make notes of the dates you've had on your score-card** so that you'll easily remember them once you're back in the safety of your own home. For example 'John, 52, leather trousers, get away from me, you freak'

6. **Don't be afraid to tick 'friend' instead of 'date'.** No one actually ticks 'date' - don't fall for this ploy. Mostly you will be ticking 'No' or 'No fucking way'.

7. **Now sit back and wait for the phone calls.** I think there's something wrong with my phone. No, there's definitely a dial tone.

PLENTY OF FISH?

In summer 2012, I met Derek, a 44-year-old IT Technician. He seemed OK by email, but on the phone I could tell that he was a major geek. Not that I mind geeks, I quite like them, but I hate to compete! After I told him I'd seen a great geek T-Shirt online ('There are 10 types of people in the world...those that understand binary and those that don't.') he had to go one better, he asked what the greatest number was that you could count to on 10 fingers. Then, in order, I assume, to try and impress me, answered his own question (1023). God, I hate that.

Anyway, I agreed to meet up with him for a pub lunch.
The conversation didn't come easily, and I found myself asking most of the questions. Half an hour in, I was struggling. Whenever I made a comment, he had to go one better. I mentioned that my dog had had an injury superglued when he went to the vet, and Derek then told me the entire history of superglue. 'Actually superglue was originally created for that purpose.' (Yeah. I know) Tedious.

We discussed past dates, well actually I discussed past dates, but I think I finally found a subject he couldn't one-up me on. I told him if I had my way some of my previous dates would have their balls shot off. He said his balls were safe as he had a metal plate in them! Then listed in the places in his body where he had metal plates inserted from when he suffered a cycling injury. It was a nice dinner table conversation.

At one point he said 'So tell me about the love of your life' and when I started to talk openly about the 'one that got away', he said that he had meant my dog.

I was glad when I could finally get away. He seemed quite keen, surprisingly enough, seeing as we didn't have anything in common. But I will not be seeing him again, and I thank my lucky stars I shall not be making acquaintance with his metal plated balls!

2-HOUR MAN

Summer 2011

I don't remember his name, but he clearly thought he was Vince Vaughn. Tall, dark-haired and arrogant. Another internet date, we'd agreed to meet at a pub near St Albans - a long way for me to go for a complete let-down. He turned up late and seemed disappointed to see me. We took a table away from the bar and I could just tell it was going to be awful. He told me about some of his previous nightmare dates - one woman had apparently chased his car down the street after their date - clearly she must have forgotten her guide dog.

Now this part I remember clearly...he said it didn't matter whether he got on with a girl or not, he would always give the date 2 hours of his time. I felt like saying 'How generous of you!' but I held my tongue. Oh God! I was going to have to put up with this jerk for longer than I had hoped.
After 2 hours had passed (he checked his watch) he finally made his excuses by saying something like 'Must get up early tomorrow for work,' and he added 'And you have had your 2 hours!'
Yes, I certainly had.

I refrained from chasing his car down the street.

GROPEY MAN

November 2009

Phil was a little older than me and worked as an engineering manager for a Telecoms company. We met through an online dating agency and he had actually taken the time to phone me to ask me where I fancied going to eat. How nice. I told him my favourite food was Thai and suggested some really good Thai restaurants in the little town where we were meeting. I was quite looking forward to a nice Thai meal and a bit of male attention, so imagine my surprise when we meet up and he's very thoughtfully booked a table at the Cafe Uno.

I was willing to overlook the disappointment of not being able to order a portion of the Tod Man Pla and a Beef Panang (I had the gnocchi) as although Phil wasn't that attractive, he seemed relatively chatty and not at all put off by the fact that I wasn't Claudia Schiffer. So we chatted for a while and I eventually decided that I might even be up for a second date. The gnocchi was horrible and left a bad taste in my mouth – perhaps an omen of what was to come. And there started the bizarre second half of the date...

Phil suggested moving on to a local hotel bar to continue our chat, so off we went. At the hotel bar he went into detail of his past dates and mentioned that one of the women he'd dated happened to be friends with another woman he'd also had a date with, and apparently it was suggested that they all have a threesome. (Oh dear, I know where this is going) So he goes into graphic detail of his threesome with these 2 women and then asks me 'Would you be up for that?' At that moment I mentally crossed him off the 'potential second date' list.

On our way back to my car he cornered me for a kiss, which turned into more of a grope, which he seemed to want to take further. I mentioned that I liked to get to know someone first before having sex with them. He said he liked to have sex first, in order to get to know someone. And so we were at an impasse.

I declined the option of the second date, pushed him back at arm's length, and said my goodbyes.

FREAK DATING

Me and my friend Sue have been speed dating 4 or 5 times in the last few years. I'm not exactly sure what Sue thinks she is going to gain from this exercise, as I have told her time and time again that nice, normal men don't need to go speed dating, so it is unlikely that we will find one there. Still, she is an optimist. I, however, am always in need of new material for my comedy writing, and so I am up for anything. The way the evening goes is always the same - Sue and I arrive early to register, and then watch as the parade of mostly mutants file in and start building their courage with copious amounts of alcohol. We stand at the bar, I grimace, put my hand in the air and shout 'Taxi!' And so it begins...5 minutes of hell with each lucky contestant.

Here are some of the highlights (but mostly lowlights):

Oil Rig Man - He had turned up looking unwashed, in dirty clothes and clearly had made no effort. He bored everyone senseless by talking about oil pipe lines for the full 5 minutes and never asked a single question. Had he been the last man on earth, I'd have been trying to repopulate the planet with part-human-part-cactus children.

The Hotty - we'll call him Ben - Sue and I got chatting to this really nice guy at the second speed dating event - he was the only cute one in the room - and he seemed genuine too, with a great sense of humour. We got around to discussing previous speed dating encounters. We were having a whale of a time telling Ben all about 'oil rig man' and how he had bored us with his tales of pipelines and so on. Eventually we asked Ben what he did for a living. He said he worked on an oil rig. Oh how we laughed and laughed, until we realised that he was actually being serious. Shit! Never did get his number.

Married Man - the age range of the event was 30 - 45, and this guy was clearly in his 60s. He was smarmy and creepy, like a lechier Leslie Philips. He moved his chair right up next to me, telling me that he really wanted to go for a coffee with Sue. He said that most of the men at the event were probably married, and asked how I felt about that. Terrific, obviously. I'd paid £15 for this. He asked me if I'd go out with someone who was married or still living with their wife (clearly he was still living with his wife). I said 'No'. He seemed put-out with that answer. He never asked a single question about me.

Scary Ed – he was an older man who looked like a cross between Herman Munster and Alistair Darling. He wore a leather waistcoat and leather trousers - which must have been his special 'dating' outfit, as when we saw him at another speed dating event, months later, he was wearing the same thing. He didn't seem to like anything very much, especially small talk. He actually said 'I don't do small talk'. Which was fine for me, as I just launched into my 'how do you feel about 'Heisenberg's uncertainty principle'? material. He said he was trying speed dating in order to look for (and this is verbatim) 'the generic things that everyone else is looking for in our culture.' So a shag then?

Exotic Sam – he had just had a date-ette with Sue when he got around to me, and spent the entire 5 minutes asking me about her restaurant preferences. Why hadn't he just asked her? He was of European origin (can't remember where from – Mediterranean somewhere) and not bad looking and had decided he absolutely had to go on a date with Sue, no matter what. I told him that her favourite restaurant was probably Italian. He ended up asking her out and took her to a Harvester on the edge of town. The romantic fool.

Sue wondered why he never seemed to answer his phone during the evenings, and why he paid at the restaurant with cash.... hmmm. When questioned about his lack of phone availability, he said defensively 'I'm not married if that's what you mean.' Sue, quite rightly, dumped him.

Slightly Effeminate Shirley - Was this his real name? No idea. He seemed to be gay. He said he wanted to 'write a novel or a poem for his children' (currently non existent children). But he hoped to have both children and writing ability by the time he passed on. Optimistic.

The Swimming German - Apparently he complained to Sue that there were no outdoor swimming pools in the UK (there are!) and then he ran off while he was chatting to her, coming back after 2 minutes with no explanation.

The Racist Algerian - During his 5 minutes with Sue, he told her that he was black and she was white - he was very observant - and complained that Slough was full of Asians, that he didn't like dating where he worked because 'all the women are black and wear trainers'. During my 5 minutes with him, I asked him what he did for a living - he said 'I work in women's clothing' - I said 'Do people look at you strangely when you say that?' but not even a smile out of him for that one. Humourless.

The Professor - Larry - had a mad beard, looked like he belonged at the Open University circa 1974. He was a scientist, studying effects of pollutants and heavy metals on something or other (as my brain had stopped listening by the time he'd finished that sentence) When quizzed about what kind of science he liked, he said 'all'. So I asked him whether he was interested in quantum physics (my usual trick). He said he wasn't clever enough to know anything about that. I said nothing. There's a time and place for Heisenberg's Uncertainly Principle. This wasn't it.

Chicken Korma Guy – Told me he used to work as a courier. He bored me senseless as he had nothing to say for himself and his only anecdotes involved food. One involved a Tesco takeaway containing (he listed these): a Ken Hom Kung Po Chicken (he called it a Ko Po chicken), special fried rice (with peas) (yes, he actually specified the 'with peas' bit) and then he repeated the conversation again, as if I hadn't heard it the first time around. Was this a good time to bring up 'Heisenberg's Uncertaintly Principle'? I thought not. His best anecdote concerned a chicken korma and an incident in a Hungry Horse Pub. He had ordered a chicken korma, and the naan bread had been too hard. When the landlady had come around to ask him if everything was alright with his meal his said 'No, this naan bread is very hard' - at the same time banging said naan bread on the side of the plate and tipping the whole thing on the floor. Ahhhh good times! The only note I wrote about him at the end of the night was 'Nightmare. Go away please.'

The Boy Next Door - David was your typical boy-next-door type, only not quite as attractive. Looked a bit like Joe 90. So really he was more of the-boy-next-door-but-one type. He was a bit geeky, and wore glasses, but he was friendly and chatty and came to talk to me and Sue after the speed dating was over. So, we were prepared to give him a chance. We had a bit of a laugh reminiscing with him about the local weirdoes (women as well as men, it turned out) for he had as many stories to tell about these women as we had about the men. He said that one woman had told him she only dated men with dogs. He said he used to have a dog but it died, so she had quizzed him, suspiciously, on the nature of the dog's death. The fact that he didn't currently own a living dog seemed to go against him. But it didn't matter, he said, because he had already got his sights on the 'best looking woman in the room,' (his words) which was apparently neither myself nor Sue. Charming. With a touch of Schadenfreude I smiled, as clearly this perfect woman wasn't the least bit interested in Joe 90 or anyone else within the vicinity. Happily, everyone left as they had arrived....still single, and stupidly optimistic that their Mr (or Miss) Right was definitely out there somewhere.

MY (NOT VERY) FUNNY VALENTINE

February 2014

It's not very often that I receive a Valentine's Day card, but surprisingly this year I did, and for about 5 minutes (the time it took from picking it up from the mail room, until opening in my office) I was actually pretty thrilled, thinking it might actually be from someone I fancied. But dear readers, this is reality, and not a Tom Hanks / Meg Ryan movie, unfortunately, and it's never the ones you fancy that send you Valentine's cards, is it? Inside the card was written something along the lines of 'Dear Sharon, Happy Valentine's Day, love from your ardent admirer. If you're interested in hearing more, call me on ***********'.   My heart sank. I knew exactly who it was from. Alan. This was a guy that I had met online about 10 years ago and chatted to briefly - we'd arranged to go on a date, but he had cancelled and I was never bothered enough about him to re-arrange. I knew it was from him because he is the only person I ever knew (from a previous Valentine's card) to use the word 'ardent'. Plus he'd been requesting my friendship on Facebook recently- and I'd turned him down each time. Some people just don't get the message!

I was surprised to have heard from him after all this time - clearly he was fixated! Or desperate. Or both.

I never phoned the number he left me, but about a week later started getting blocked number calls at strange hours, which I didn't pick up. Finally today, while I was at work, I got a text message from a different number:

Him: Hi Sharon, how's you? What u upto these days...Met the man of your dreams yet?! X
Me: Who is this?   (I knew exactly who it was)
Him: It's Al.
Me: Al who? (evil LOL)
Him: Went on a date a few years ago. (No we didn't)
Me: Where did we go?
Him: ****** where you lived.
Me: Sorry I don't remember

(Any normal person at this time would have given up, right?   Not Captain Desperation though.)

Him: No probs. So have you found Mr. Right then?
Me: Yes, thank you for asking. (I hadn't, I was trying to get rid of him)
Him: Is that yes you have met someone? (Are you stupid or something?)
Me: Yes

Him: So can't interest you in a beer sometime then? (I don't drink beer)
Me: No thanks

Oh just get over it will you? Clearly I am just so completely unforgettable! I might be flattered if he'd ever actually met me.

NOT MAGIC MIKE

In 2007 I briefly moved to Devon and met Mike on an online dating agency site. On his profile he had lied about his age, saying he was in his mid-forties, when in fact he was 50. Still, I didn't mind as I believe age is pretty irrelevant when you really like someone, younger or older. For me, it's more about what we have in common, their personality and sense of humour.

Our first date was a drink and snack at a seaside restaurant, but I was too nervous to eat, which is unlike me. I was so worried about whether he liked me or not, as I immediately liked him and wondered if a relationship would develop. He was handsome and well-mannered and we seemed to have a few things in common.

Luckily it seemed we both felt the same way, and he too wanted to have a second date. Inevitably that all led to The 3rd Date (we all know what the 3rd date means!) and Mike came round for dinner and dessert (!) at my house. I don't remember much about the actual night itself, but I do remember that Mike had a little problem. Ahem. He couldn't get it up. And because of this issue, also refused to use protection.

But even with the lack of a decent time in the sack, I was blissfully happy being with Mike. After having not been in a proper relationship for over 3 years, it made a nice change. I was starting to think he could be The One.

Four weeks later, there came a bolt from the blue. It was a Sunday morning, Mike had popped over and I was expecting us to spend the day together, making pasties or something appropriately Devon-ish. (What is the Devon equivalent of 'Cornish'?)   But he had other plans. He sat me down on the sofa and said 'I don't see our relationship going anywhere.' But he explained that he didn't want to stop seeing me completely. And without stopping to find out if I was OK, he left.

I remember taking the dog out in the pouring rain and crying my eyes out for the whole day, and some of the Monday morning at work. I cried so much, I haven't been able to properly cry since.

Mike and I did see each other again, one more time, as I'd invited him to a family do, and he didn't want to let me down. But I felt like it was a bit pointless and I hated introducing him to my family - was he my 'boyfriend' or was he something else?

Two months later just as I was getting over him, my phone rang. It was him. I was suddenly stupidly thrilled, thinking he had reconsidered and wanted me back, but no. He'd met someone else. Was this just before he broke up with me? It sounded like it. Why was he telling me this? It turns out they'd already had sex (and why was he telling me that?) but she was concerned and refused to sleep with him again until she knew he was STD free. He said that at her request, he'd had an HIV test, but that he wanted me to have one to reassure his new girlfriend. Cheeky fucker! Mr 'I won't wear condoms' was asking me to help him get laid by someone else.

Then he started asking me about my past sexual relationships. Had I ever slept with anyone that I might have contracted anything from? I didn't quite know what to say, I was still in complete confusion over why he'd called to ask me this. I mischievously considered lying and saying 'well there was that gang bang with a ship load of Somali pirates...' but the seriousness of the moment got the better of me. I coolly told him I'd think about it, meaning of course 'No fucking way, knobhead'

Anyway, I hope she had as good a time in the sack with him, as I'd had.

THE ONE WHERE I GET MY REVENGE ON AN EVIL HENCHMAN

Back around 1999, in my very early days of internet dating, at the time when I very naively believed everything a man told me - 'I'm not married' / 'I really like you' / 'I'm looking for a serious relationship' / 'Your bum doesn't look big in that' - I met Mark. He was a stunt man and proudly showed off the fact that he had been in a Bond Film. So I watched it (again) and there he was. Man alive! He actually was in a Bond film - as an Evil Henchman.

We had drinks at a pub not too far from my home, and he was honest enough to tell me that he had 2 children and was therefore still living with his ex wife. I was sympathetic to his situation - he and his ex didn't get on, but were making the best of things for the sake of the children. He said he hadn't told his ex he was coming out dating (as he didn't want to upset her) and had said that he had told her instead that he was meeting his friend 'Dave'.

We got on well, and made arrangements to see each other again sometime. In the meantime we exchanged a few emails, and cheekily, as a little joke, I always signed off 'Dave'.

On our 2nd date he came over to my place for dinner, and wasn't content to wait on the '3rd date rule'. He made it quite clear that he wanted to sleep with me. I told him I didn't think it was a good idea, that I didn't just want to have sex with him and then for him to run off as soon as he got it, but he was adamant - he wasn't going anywhere. It was fine. I said Ok.

As expected he went straight off the radar as soon as he got what he wanted, but the best part was still to come. For me anyway, if not for him. I caught him online a couple of weeks later and asked him what had happened - he said (get this) he thought I was being 'too clingy'. If assuming that a man will still want to hang around after he's had sex (like he promised he would) is 'clingy', then yes I was 'clingy'. Fuckwit.

I rolled my eyes. I had dodged a bullet there. But there was more to come.

A few days later I got an instant chat message from a woman I didn't know. The message just read 'Why Dave?' Being the quick-witted, sharp sort of girl I am, I immediately knew that this must be Mark's so-called 'ex' wife. Clearly not an 'ex' at all. She had obviously been going through his emails, had found mine and wondered who I was. She had checked out my online profile and could see I was a woman called Sharon, and not a 'Dave' at all.

I thought fast, and after a few internet tweaks replied with this message. 'Hi, sorry but Dave is my flatmate, he often uses my email address. But you can find him at Dave....@aol.com.' In the meantime, I had created an email address and online presence for 'Dave', along with a profile. Dave's profile went sometime like this:

Name: Dave.....
Sexual Orientation: Gay.
Job: Airline steward.
Interests: kinky sex, being submissive, Barbra Streisand music. (Or something along those lines)

Talk your way out of that one, fuckwit!! I grinned smugly and wished Mark a pleasant evening with his wife.
There is a moral to this story, but it has temporarily slipped my devious little mind.

THE FANTASY DATE

03/03/2014

A couple of days ago, my very good friend, Imogen asked me the question that I'd usually expect to hear from a man. 'What is your fantasy?' She didn't quite mean it in the same way that a guy would mean it, though she probably expected me to say 'Benedict Cumberbatch, a set of handcuffs and a jar of Nutella.'

Going slightly off subject for just a moment, I've had some pretty funny questions from guys over the years...(apart from the one about Marwell zoo) ...the usual 'What are you wearing?' to which I always reply 'scuba gear', or 'Where are your hands?' 'on a biscuit,' and my all-time favourite, from a troublesome online pest, 'What would you do if you were locked in a room with me?' 'I'd claw my way out with my bare hands.' Him: 'LOL. yeah, but seriously?' Me: 'Seriously'.

Anyway, so Imogen had asked 'What is your fantasy?' she explained that what she actually meant was 'What is your fantasy date with [the man you currently have in your sights]?' I had to tell her the truth... my fantasy was this... 'I just want to go on a normal date with a normal guy.'

52

I have had so many bad dates I've begun to wonder if all dates are like mine - but from what they tell me, my friends have had slightly more successful meet-ups than me - dates which don't usually end up being the subject of hilarious after-dinner conversations and cringe-worthy online blogs. (Ok, some of them do.) But some of them have actually had dates that resulted in relationships. Whereas my last long-term relationship was 10 years ago.

And it's not as if I have unrealistic expectations, I don't expect marriage (I already nearly made that mistake - the dress was bought, the church booked - after a 5-year engagement, at 24 I had finally had enough and had grown the balls to walk away) and I was never bothered about having children. I would be perfectly happy cooking dinner for a guy once a week, having some fun in the sack, and him going home, if that's what made him happy.

I value my independence and though I spend a lot of time on my own, I'm seldom lonely - I like my own company. So, I am in no way desperate either. And despite the cynicism that these terrible experiences have left me with, I am still a romantic fool. When I'm around someone I'm attracted to, my legs still turn to jelly, my words refuse to come out in a logical order, and I get hopelessly clumsy – for example, recently I very nearly poked out the eye of a man I fancied with a pencil as I gesticulated excitedly in his presence.

I am useless at knowing when someone is attracted to me. Subtlety doesn't really work with me. One day, a few years ago, I suddenly got the impression a young colleague was trying to chat me up. I couldn't quite believe it (he was quite a catch) I had a rabbit-in-the-headlights moment and later I wished I'd said something encouraging, and not the equivalent of 'I carried a watermelon'.

Who would I like to date? Some people have a check list a mile long, but not me. I don't rule out people because of age or height or whether or not they regularly get mistaken for Hugh Jackman. He must be non-smoking and have a great sense of humour, but that is where the checklist ends. Oh, and it would help if he actually liked women.

So what about me? What do I have to give? Well, I'm happy, intelligent, honest, loyal, loving, generous to a fault and have a fantastic sense of humour. I'm genuinely interested in people and what they think, and I'm sympathetic to their feelings. I refuse to act my age. Unfortunately, in my head I'm still 25, though my wobbly bits may tell otherwise! I'm a great cook, and not only great in the kitchen but other rooms as well.

My Italian side gives me passion and a bit of a temper, but it takes a lot for me to lose it - I've only ever lost it 3 times in
my life - I'm usually such a contented soul, that it tends to shock people. I've grown philosophical with age and am much more 'live and let live' than I used to be. The down side is I get bored easily and have to be constantly mentally stimulated (luckily my job gives me this) but it can be quite a challenge (one of the reasons I like to write.)

I've given dating a wide berth for the last couple of years, as I felt I was at the end of my tether with it. Internet dating was all too shallow for my liking - I hope, dear reader, that you never have to experience walking into a bar to meet your date and seeing the look on their face drop in disappointment. Dates like that do nothing to bolster my already flagging confidence, and just make me want to misbehave and have a little fun at their expense - sometimes I am a little devil...

...Like with the guy I'd arranged to meet in a pub in Berkshire, who couldn't stand me from the first moment he saw me. He was 15 minutes late, never offered to buy me a drink, acted like a complete prick throughout and never gave me a chance. I was determined to torture him just a little - I started by ordering food - he didn't order anything. I even had to buy him a drink!

He worked in IT, or something like that, and he clearly thought he was something special.
I asked him what job he would have if he could do something interesting (dig!). He said he'd be a novelist or be in a band. So I asked him what instrument he played - he told me he didn't play an instrument (optimistic!) So then I asked him what he wrote - he said he hadn't written anything. So I told him I'd written 2 novels. There's nothing like a dose of reality for the simple minded, is there? At the end of the date, which lasted only 45 minutes, he left, and I've never seen a man run so fast.

So when it comes to dating men, I have little expectation. A man could impress me just by showing up, being nice to me and listening. That is the fantasy. Anything else is just the icing on the cake.

ABOUT TIME

04/03/2014

A couple of weeks ago I was watching the movie 'About Time'. For those of you that haven't seen it, it's about a guy who discovers he can travel back in time within his own lifetime and change things that have happened to him. So as you can imagine, it lends itself to some pretty funny situations, for example, as he perfects his first sexual experience with his new love interest. But wait a minute, for this isn't just your standard rom-com. There's a very philosophical and serious side to the story - for in changing just one aspect of his earlier life, the 'ripple effect' (stay with me here) completely alters his life from that point on, to the present day.

So, I got to wondering (in the manner of *Sex and the City*'s Carrie Bradshaw) If you could go back and alter just one thing in your life, what would it be? And how would changing it impact your present?   Now, I don't think it's healthy to have too many regrets in life...Every mistake, every disappointment, and failure is a valuable learning experience. (If you disagree, try blogging, it's cheaper than therapy!)

I believe that people come into your life to teach you some sort of lesson, and once that lesson is learned, they leave, and there's nothing you can do about that, painful as it is. I also believe that everything happens for a reason, even the really shitty stuff. For example, if I hadn't had the kind of love life that would have made weaker people want to take a shotgun and blow their own brains out, I wouldn't have any of these round-the-camp-fire type anecdotes to amuse my friends with. Every cloud, as they say...
But if I had my chance again, I know the one thing that I would seriously consider changing...
As alluded to previously in this book, from the age of 19 to 24, I was engaged to Will. Will and I met at work. He was 5 years older than me, had already had a previous long term relationship, but was my first boyfriend. There were other guys at work that I liked too, but Will was the one to ask me out.

Back in those days I was very shy and naive and I had no idea what to expect from a relationship. What I hadn't expected was that in order to spend any time with him, I'd have to accompany him to every basketball game across the London area, while he refereed, and every motor racing event at Brands Hatch, as he marshalled.

I remember that most of our relationship was taken up by me doing things that he wanted to do, and never the other way around. I even had to holiday where he wanted - this meant learning to ski. I hated it from the first second. It was freezing, I caught a cold. My scarf froze to my face. I'd never experienced what minus 26 degrees felt like before. Will left me in ski school on the nursery slopes each morning, while he went off skiing on his own. At one point during a lesson, I took a bad fall, somehow somersaulting into a ditch and damaging my hip. This to me was no holiday. Our second skiing holiday was much the same, but this time I wasn't in ski school. I still had a cold. It still hurt. And I still hated it. During the 5 years we spent together he never once asked me where I'd like to go - I was left in no doubt, it was never even an option.

To say that Will was selfish would have been an understatement. I remember one evening sitting in the living room of my house, watching my telly with Will by my side. The news was on. I tried to start a conversation and was immediately shot down and silenced.... 'When the TV's on, that means I'm watching it!' (Verbatim.)

If I'd have been the person I am now and he'd have said that to me, the telly lead would have been yanked out of the wall and he'd have had to have his balls surgically removed from the roof of his mouth. But, dear reader, I was the kind of doormat that just let it slide. I took the shit, I kept my mouth shut.

Will was hardly ever around. If he wasn't working, he had plenty of other extra-curricular activities to keep him busy. Not just the basketball refereeing, or the motor-racing marshalling, but he was also a Royal Naval Reservist. The Navy would take him away for a few weeks once a year for training, and it was during one of these that my grandmother unfortunately passed away. When I really needed him, he just wasn't there.

After our long engagement, it was time to start planning the wedding. My heart wasn't really in it, but I felt pulled along by the inevitability of it all. I had no desire to hurt him, or either of our families, by wimping-out and breaking-up with him. I felt like I'd be letting people down. So the church was booked, the dress was bought and the reception venue chosen. But I was miserable.

It was during this wedding-planning period - yet another lonely evening in without Will - that I was watching 'Four Weddings and a Funeral'. Hugh Grant was in the same situation as me. He didn't love his intended, he loved somebody else. I suddenly had something resembling a 'eureka' moment. I realised that I didn't have to go ahead with the wedding. I'd finally got to that place where I knew I'd had enough. Will arrived home that night and I was in floods of tears. I told him I couldn't marry him. He said it was alright, we didn't have to get married. And I said No, he hadn't understood, it wasn't just that I didn't want to get married, but I didn't want to be with him any longer. Soon afterwards he moved out. Hurting him was the hardest thing I've ever had to do.

I had spent 5 years of my young life with someone who didn't really love me. He might have thought at the time that he did, but he didn't. I would never be his number one priority, and probably not even number 2 either. Luckily, I didn't really love him either, but it had taken me a while to work that out.
For some reason I never lost my 'V plates' to Will. Maybe I was just never that attracted to him. That might sound strange to a lot of people, to spend 5 years in an intimate relationship with someone and not have sex, but I wasn't ready, and I wanted to save it for someone I actually loved. And I did.

Luckily, Will found his match and got married a long time ago, but he still kept in contact. I remember when I first joined Facebook and uploaded a few photos of all my old friends from work...the tagging thing was all new to me, but I logged on the next morning to find that Will had tagged all my photos of all my friends. I was seething.   He still hadn't relinquished control.

Recently I took the decision to remove him from my Facebook friends. I thought it was healthier.

Well, that story was pretty long-winded, but we got there in the end...So, the one thing I think I would change if I could, would be that I would say 'No' to Will, when he asked me out. And I wouldn't have wasted what could have been the best 5 years of my life.

But how would that one change 'ripple' forwards to my life now? If I had said 'No' and given someone else a chance, maybe I'd be married, divorced, have a couple of kids, maybe I wouldn't have been able to travel all over the world like I have, seen the ancient wonders, marvel at the strangeness and magnificence of our little planet, not met some of the fantastic people I've met, the great friends, colleagues and students, maybe I'd have a different job, one I didn't enjoy, or no job at all.

I wouldn't be the person that I am now if I had altered even one little thing. In short, that one word changed my life.

So, dear reader, I ask again...what would you change?

LOVE IN A PARALLEL UNIVERSE

07/03/2014

Last week, my boss told me that he wished he could clone me. (Of course they were bound to find some way of making me work 24 hours a day with no extra pay.) Very flattering, but if given the choice, would I decline the offer? Could I pass off all the shitty jobs to Sharon II? And maybe make her go on all my blind dates for me? This is all completely hypothetical of course. Or is it?

Imagine my surprise when, back in 1999 or thereabouts, I turned up at the TV production company where I worked, for a late shift and found out that I was already there! Or rather my 'doppelganger' was already there. I didn't get to see the other me, but was assured by the now frightened receptionist that I had come in at 8am that morning, without saying a word to her, and had made my way to the TV studio. I told her that if I was already in, that I was going to go back home and back to bed. But she didn't see the funny side. (I do so hate when my clever jokes fall flat!)

She was quite visibly shaken and so I believed her strange account. This rated about an 11 on the weird-shit-o-meter. (Actually it didn't surprise me too much, as I have so many paranormal experiences, I could probably write a book on that as well.) You hear about people 'searching' for themselves but this was an entirely new take on that idea. I looked for myself all day but never found me. (That's the first and only time you will ever see that sentence in print. I can guarantee it.) (I am totally original!) (Apart from my doppelganger.) I wondered if this doppelganger had a better life than me - the answer was 'probably not' because she was clearly working in the same shit hole that I was. Was she the perfect size 10? No, apparently she'd been wearing the same clothes as I was wearing that day too. Did she have a better love life? (Let's face it, she couldn't have had a worse one.) Who was she? Was she a temporary visitor from a parallel universe? A glitch in the Matrix? Or a living ghost?

Somewhere out there, were there parallel universes all with alternate versions of Sharon? And if so, what would these alternate versions all be doing? Would Sharon III be a successful Hollywood screenwriter?

Had Sharon IV discovered the secret to eternal youth? Was Sharon V a successful model-slash-actor, currently dating Benedict Cumberbatch? And Sharon VI a supreme marksman and assassin for hire? Would my luck with men have been any better with an alternate version of me? Probably. Let's see...

...Sharon V definitely would have had more confidence with the opposite sex. She wouldn't have taken any shit from her friend and long-time crush, 'Dave', unlike me... I had offered to drive him home from a party when he was a little worse for wear. He'd said 'I'm so drunk I could even sleep with you right now'. Sharon V would have pulled the car to a halt, pushed him out, drove off to the nearest bar, and pulled the hottest man in there. She would not have carried on driving, dropped him home and felt bad about herself for the rest of eternity.

When faced with Scott, the (married it turned out) man who led her on and continued a lie for 6 months, would Sharon VI have just given up and walked away, defeated and disillusioned with love? No, she would have hunted the bastard down and made sure he never did it to some other poor, unsuspecting soul.
And Sharon IV, faced with a come-on from her young, hot colleague, would have followed up and asked him to dinner.

But alas, I am nothing like those alternate versions of myself. I am just the product of my experiences in this universe, good and bad. Maybe I'll never be a hired assassin, or a model / actor dating Benedict Cumberbatch, but I like who I am, and there's always potential for successes in the fields where my talents lie. I am lucky, my friends and family love me just the way I am. I don't have to be anyone else.

So would I clone me? No. She'd be too much competition.

CRAZY STUPID LOVE

09/03/2014

Earlier this week, my friend Imogen sprung a wedding invitation on me - she needed a 'plus-one'. I'm not usually one for weddings, but I said Yes and jumped to her rescue - not only because she's one of my best friends but because I'd also had occasion to call on her services as a 'plus-one' in the past. (By the way, you know you're a lost cause when the 'plus-one' on your invite is your dog!)

After a 2-hour journey to Gloucestershire, we found the church and took a seat at the back, as Imogen has a tendency to burst into fits of giggles in serious situations. (As her optician can testify.)   The wedding ceremony itself was actually one of the best ones I've been to - the vicar was lovely, had a great sense of humour, and had his own stand-up thing going. And we recognised 66% of the hymns (that's 2 out of 3 for anyone not so good at maths) - I don't think the vicar had ever heard 'All Things Bright and Beautiful' sung with such vigour (or fits of giggles.)

Anyway, the vicar talked a lot about Love and Cupid's Arrow (the happy couple had met while taking archery lessons) (so, must sign up for some of those!) There was the popular reading from 1- Corinthians - chapter 13 - 'If I speak in the tongues of mortals and of angels, but do not have love, I am a noisy gong or a clanging cymbal ...' etc. And I got to thinking about love. Crazy, Stupid Love.

The reading goes on to say 'Love is patient, love is kind...Love never fails.' Wonderful for those who experience it in that way, but in my own experience love has been none of those things. Love can be complicated, inconvenient, painful, heartbreaking and messy. In my so-called 'Love life' I have been: messed around, cheated on, lied to, taken advantage of, and generally not treated very nicely. But that doesn't mean that I have lost all faith in love.

I'm the type of person who falls in love quite easily, once I'm in a relationship. I let my heart rule my head and I jump right in with both eyes firmly closed. Not always the best of ideas, and I have been hurt by falling for guys who have no intention of returning the favour. Maybe this is why I have avoided getting emotionally entangled for so long. How can you tell when someone loves you back?

Recently I began to get strange vibes from someone I've been spending a bit of time with, and I started to sense that he might have developed a bit of a crush on me. He is the only person that I have noticed flirting with me in years. My spidey senses have never been very good on this, but a couple of people, including my friend, have also noticed how he behaves around me, so I know I'm not going mad. At first I didn't want to think about it, I was perfectly content being single and not having the rollercoaster ride of romance to deal with. But as I got more used to the idea, it was nice to feel like I was special to someone. What can I say? I'm a sucker for love, even though it completely screws with everything.

So, who is this guy? Like I'm going to tell you! I would never want to do anything to embarrass him. Well, what's he like? I can honestly say that he's one of the nicest men I've ever met - over the short time I have got to know him, I have found that he is always considerate, polite, respectful, and interested.

He's also funny, intelligent and handsome. He has come to my 'rescue' on a couple of occasions in the last few weeks and for that he is my absolute hero. I wonder what he sees in me, and whether this is just a crush or something more.

So, why do I not make a move? (What, with MY history?) It's true I have been stupidly brave in the past and actually asked people out or told them how I felt about them - 9 times out of 10 I have been shot down in flames.

My worst experience of this was around 1996 when I liked a guy at work called Adam. He was constantly flirting with me, but never made a move, so being completely chicken, I got my sister to ask him how he felt. Turns out he liked me as a friend, but nothing more. A few days after this, my colleague and good friend Dave (yes, I've mentioned him on here before) got wind of this, and he waited until the moment was right...until just him, Adam and I were in the same room together. Dave said 'So, Adam, you like Sharon just as friends but nothing more?' he then walked out of the room, leaving me alone with Adam. The bastard.

I gave up asking people out several years ago. If a man's interested, he'll come to you, or so I've been told. But with this one there is a complication, actually there are 3, so I can't ask him anyway. The ball is firmly in his court.

It's extremely frustrating. And it's at times like these, where I have nothing to lose, that the phrase 'Carpe Diem' (Seize the Day) comes into my head, and reminds me that sometimes love requires a leap of faith. It takes one person to be brave. And I have always believed that if you really like someone, you should tell them. Screw the consequences. Unless they're married, of course, or gay, or a homicidal maniac.

So here I am being brave (or stupid) with no hope or agenda, and simply inviting him in, if that is what he wants. If it isn't what he wants, then nothing is lost, and I wish him the very best of luck, for he deserves it. At best, maybe he'll ask me out, and at worst, I hope he'll just be flattered. But all I'm expecting is nothing.

VEGGIES & STALKERS & LODGERS, OH MY!

10/03/2014

My love life has become a bit of a running joke to my friends and family. My dad always calls anyone that I date a 'victim', as in 'Who's your latest victim?' - like I'm some kind of vampire, about to drain them of their will to live, probably by questioning them on their knowledge of quantum physics and the nature of reality (I don't really do that.) (Unless I dislike them.)   As my last 3 long-term relationships were with (by complete coincidence) vegetarians, my parents always want to check 'He's not another vegetarian, is he?' And my friends always know that they are going to be in for a laugh as soon as I tell them the latest date news.   I am like the CNN of terrible dates. I should get one of those 24 hour news headline 'tickers' crawling across my chest. '.....Sharon knees randy Frenchman in the nuts....' etc.

A couple of years ago my sister and her husband tried to set me up with one of her husband's karate mates, Shaun. They even produced a little 'dating profile' for me and gave it to Shaun.

Apparently Shaun recognised me immediately, and asked if I was 'the same Sharon who was in to all that paranormal stuff'. I was the same Sharon.

It turns out that I had already been on a date with this man, arranged through a dating agency site. Unbelievable. (I'd had a case of Déjà who?) Clearly I had already dated most of the single men in Britain, so it was bound to happen at some point!
I couldn't remember much about Shaun, except that we had met up at a bar in Watford. I had no memory of him at all. So it can't have been a great date, but then again, it can't have been as bad as most of the other ones, either.

But it's not only me that's had some bad dating experiences... My friend Imogen has unfortunately had a few of her own lately - her last 2 boyfriends started stalking her. I told her to send one my way. (One of them just hacked her Facebook account last night and 'fraped' her, putting her status as 'I have a magical vajayjay and enormous boobies!' I am trying not to laugh out loud, really I am.)

On the subject of stalking, a couple of years ago, a very cute colleague of mine, on receiving my address in an email I sent him, stated that he could now 'come and hide behind [my] hedge'.

I told him I didn't have a hedge. Of all the fecking stupid things to say! I kicked myself for that one for months. Now that I've moved house, I do actually have a hedge, if that offer still stands...

But I have had bad experiences of stalking too. One was when I was about 26. His name was Dino, he was also part Italian and interested in the paranormal, but that was the limit of our things-in-common. Unfortunately he thought he was Fox Mulder (from the 'X Files') and he wanted me to be his 'Dana Scully'. He had taped an 'X' in his kitchen window (the sad fucker) and had also named his cat 'Dana.' We didn't exactly date, we just went for a couple of days out, and I really wasn't interested in him romantically. However, he was crazy about me. Why is that always the way?

I invited him to a party at my house one evening and he arrived 2 hours early - obviously hoping to get some alone time with me. Luckily, my lovely ex-boyfriend, Jack, was also at my house at the time, so I wasn't left alone with Dino. The party had a cross-dressing theme, but Dino had turned up without a dress. I was annoyed to have to lend him one of mine, and even more annoyed to find it fitted him, and he looked better in it than I did. I should have told him to keep it - I couldn't bring myself to wear it again afterwards.

A few days after the party, Dino kept phoning me and leaving messages on my answerphone. I felt he was really starting to become a pest at that point. In one of the messages he said 'I know you're there, so pick up.' I got a little scared at this point and had to get my very nervous lodger, Chris, to answer it. Anyway, Chris was good enough to pick up the phone and tell Dino that I wasn't there. I made it clear to him shortly afterwards that I wasn't interested and thankfully he got the message and left me alone.

I could also write a blog on strange lodgers, going off on a tangent for just a moment. Chris was a sweetie but was quite awkward around other people. He would come downstairs from his bedroom, knock on my living room door and enter, wearing just his dressing gown. On one occasion he said 'Oh is it alright if I wear my dressing gown?' I said 'Yes Chris, I'd rather you did.' He also had a habit of writing Post-It notes to stick on the fridge, mostly to do with the contents of the other kitchen appliances. One particularly memorable one was 'NB. Chips in freezer.'

The stalkers, veggies and lodgers were actually pretty tame compared to my worst nightmares with the opposite sex, otherwise I may not feel the need to vent by writing this book.

PLEASURE & PAIN

11/03/2014

Back in 2006, I had laser surgery on my eyes (What the hell does this have to do with dating? You may well ask. Well, hold on a minute, reader, you know I always get to the point eventually, in a round about sort of way.) (Just be patient, or go and watch 'Mr. Selfridge' on catch-up instead. It was quite good this week.)

Anyway, back to the eye surgery - I'd spent many years wearing contact lenses for short sightedness. This habit cost a small fortune, and I couldn't get used to glasses, so eventually I decided enough was enough. I had been for the laser surgery consultation a few years prior but didn't want to go through with it. However, my dad and step-brother had both had it done, and after 8 years had passed and they'd had no complications, I decided that the time was right. And I was glad I did. The whole operation took less than 5 minutes, was completely painless, and straight away I had perfect vision. The recovery process was slightly painful as the lenses healed, but that was managed with pain killers and a couple of days spent asleep. Why had I waited so long to get this done? I was scared. I knew that there was going to be some pain, and I didn't know that it was going to be worth it.

My point is that you can't have pleasure without a little pain. Or, if you prefer 'Sometimes you have to wade through a mountain of shit to find a crumb of happiness'. Much like my love life. Mountain of shit? Try the Kilimanjaro of shit. (The 'Mount Everest of Shit' doesn't sound as funny) I tell you, I am expecting big things when I finally get my 'crumb of happiness.' I am expecting the whole fucking loaf. Or the bakery. Or the entire chain of Wenzels. Because I have really been through it. I feel like I have been to hell and back in the search for the fabled 'Mr Right'.

I can honestly say I have had some of the most painful dating experiences known to man (or woman). What the hell did I ever do in a previous life to deserve this?

In 2005, I met Ivan through a dating agency, and we'd arranged to meet on Valentine's Day (Awww! how romantic!) (Just wait, reader) at a pub near his home in Knebworth (Knebworth? Isn't that quite a drive from you? Yes it is, thank you for asking.) I remember being quite taken with Ivan - he was 37, charming and handsome, and he had the look of a younger Al Pacino.

He explained to me that he'd been in a terrible marriage with a bigamist, he had 2 young kids and he was looking for someone to share his life with. We got on well, and when I left that pub,

I had a bounce in my step and a sparkle in my eye. I texted him later to thank him for a lovely time, and hoped that he'd like to meet again. He texted back and said that he'd really liked me and he would definitely be up for a second date. So we arranged that he would come round to my house for dinner the following week. The lucky bastard.

The morning of the dinner date arrived and I hadn't had any contact from him for a few days, so I phoned and left a message for him, asking if he was still Ok to come. I'd bought all the ingredients, I was making the legendary breaded chicken, spaghetti with puttanesca sauce and a triple chocolate cheesecake. I treat my boyfriends very well.

I didn't hear from him until a couple of hours before he was due to arrive. He texted me. The text started with 'I've been having thoughts...' You know you're in for shit when they start 'having thoughts', don't you? (Clearly the brain had just taken over the thinking from the penis.) Ok, so what was it that he'd been 'having thoughts' about?

He wanted me to know that he really liked me but that he wanted to have a relationship with someone who would want to quickly move in with him and didn't work too far away.

I told him that it was a little early to be discussing the moving in thing, but said he shouldn't rule me out just because of that. Yes, I had my own home and job locally, but that shouldn't be an obstacle to the course of true love, should it? He seemed happy with my response, but then came back with this... 'I really like you, but I'm going to get you to a size 12, I mean that in a nice way (!) just the way I'd like to see you.' WTF? So he didn't really like me at all, he just wanted someone that he could mould into his perfect woman. This guy was a total control freak.

That stupid, shallow bastard missed out on the best goddamned cheesecake he would ever have had. It is no bloody wonder I am not a size 12, with having to eat my date's share of dinner! If I wasn't being completely messed around by men, I would be a fecking size 12. And that sodding breaded chicken has been the death knell to every date that I've ever cooked it for, but that is another story.

In 2008 I went on a date with Steve. It was another dating agency introduction. He'd looked 'good on paper' - don't they all? His profile had said that he was intelligent, had a sensational sense of humour, all that bullshit...

We met up and I don't think either one of us was that keen on the other, but we chatted and were pleasant to each other, at least. I mentioned about my interest in science and the paranormal, and he mentioned about his interest in jigsaws and photographing butterflies! Oh jeez. And sometimes he did jigsaws <u>with</u> butterflies. He got an accusatory tone in his voice as he said 'It didn't say anything in your profile about you being interested in the paranormal.' And I thought to myself 'It didn't say anything in yours about BUTTERFLIES either!'

In 2010 I met Scott, it was at the same pub in Berkshire that I'd met up with the guy that practically ran out on me, so I was having flashbacks and wasn't having high hopes for my date. It was lucky I hadn't had 'high' hopes as it turned out he wasn't much taller than me, and I'm only 5'1". He looked a bit like the actor, Tom Hollander. He was very interested to hear all about my comedy writing and wanted to read a copy of the screenplay I was working on. Fine, I said I would email it to him.

Then he told me all about his passion - in his spare time, he was a song writer and musician. He produced his CD out of his man-bag and thrust it over the table at me. Would I listen to it for him and let him know what I thought?

Who did he think I was? Simon bloody Cowell? At home later I looked it over, it was full of pretentious-sounding titles, like 'Mile High Strawberry Pie,' and 'Surroundabout'. This guy thought he was the lovechild of Lennon and McCartney. I had a listen, it was dire. I felt like Arthur Dent and Ford Prefect having to listen to Vogon poetry in 'Hitchhiker's Guide to the Galaxy'. At some point he did actually email and ask me what I thought of it. I think I got around that conversation by telling him it was 'interesting'. Just shoot me.

Each morning around 7:30am when I come in to work, I notice a single green parakeet in the tree outside our reception. He always looks pretty lonely up there all by himself on his little branch. He's been there for weeks now. But this morning I saw he'd finally got himself a little friend, who was perched right next to him, preening his feathers, kissing his little red beak. It gave me a little glow of happiness to see he'd found someone. It took him a while, but he got there in the end, and I'll bet he didn't have to date any weirdos. I have been single for a long time. I haven't had a long-term relationship in 10 years, and I haven't had my feathers preened or my beak kissed in 3 years. But that little bird gave me hope.

At least I can say that I have learned a lot from these painful experiences, and there are mistakes that I won't make again. Some of the things I've been through have it made it very difficult for me to trust men. Most of those experiences I won't be sharing in here, because there is nothing funny about them whatsoever. When you find out that someone you trusted has been lying to you, it isn't just that one lie that affects you, it's everything you're told by every other man thereafter. Love can make us blind to people's flaws and to the fact that they're arseholes. I would always say, if in doubt, trust your instincts. I didn't trust mine well enough and I paid a high price emotionally. But there are the odd one or two men that I have come to know that I would trust with my life. This is not an anti-man rant. I love men. I just don't want to be lied to by any more of them. However I wouldn't mind if one would just lie on top of me once in a while though.

I'm hoping I've now learned how to tell the good from the bad, the mentalists from the normals, and the veggies from the carnivores, and I'm finally at a place, where I can see clearly. (See what I did there?)

THE ISLAND OF LOST BOYFRIENDS

12/03/2014

(This morning, that parakeet, the one that lives in the tree outside reception at work, had got 2 little friends with him. A threesome! He is now flaunting his love life in front of me. The little shit.)

A few years ago, my best friend Amanda and I were having a bit of a mad half hour. I can't remember how this came about but was probably the result of eating too many pick 'n' mix sweets and watching the 'Sex And The City' box-set. We suddenly came up with the idea for The Island of Lost Boyfriends.

We decided that, in an ideal world, or in any sort of world that was fair and just, there should be a place where you could send your horrible ex-boyfriends. (Or girlfriends, gentlemen.) A place where they would never be able to escape. A place so terrifying, that they would rue the day that they ever meddled with our feelings.

For a laugh, we decided that we would build the island out of modeling clay. So there we were, at my kitchen table, moulding the beginnings of our little island. There was a volcano, spewing molten lava, a pit of quick sand, a palm tree full of coconuts, a T-Rex, and a pterodactyl.

We then started moulding our ex-boyfriends. It was quite strange how the model of Will, my ex-fiancé, looked exactly like him, right down to his almost invisible eyebrows and the orange motor-racing marshal's overalls, that I had decided to clothe him in. I stuck him next to the volcano, with the T-Rex peering hungrily at him.

We also moulded Nigel, my ex lodger (or 'Roger the lodger' as some of my friends had come to call him) (ahem), Scotty the RAF pilot - who was seated on top of the pterodactyl, a couple of my other ex-boyfriends, and Amanda's ex too. In total there were 6 little clay men standing on our island.

We were quite proud of our little model and left it on the kitchen table for a couple of weeks. Occasionally I'd get the urge to go and squash the models, which I did, several times. I wondered if it would have a sort of voodoo effect on them. I hoped so.

One evening during the time the Island was on show, my mother popped over. She saw the model and asked what it was. We told her. My mother said 'You don't need an island. You need a bloody continent!' She was, as ever, correct.

I wished we'd have taken a photo of the island, as it was pretty impressive, and I would have pasted it in here, but it wasn't around for long.

So, who would I have added to the Island if it were still around today?

Nicco - I never actually met Nicco in person, and I'll tell you why. I met him through a dating agency website and he seemed very nice and genuine on his profile. He was local and lived with his parents in Middlesex, and he was not at all bad looking.

We chatted on the phone, but he seemed a bit nervous. Nevertheless we arranged to meet up in a little town in Bucks for a drink. On the day of the date we texted the arrangements.
He wanted to meet outside the fish restaurant at the bottom of town, but I told him we'd have trouble parking around there. So I suggested meeting slightly further up the road at the pub, where there was plenty of parking and was right on the crossroads. But he didn't know where that was and sounded uncomfortable when I gave him the very simple directions. So we then decided that instead we'd meet in a village closer to where he lived. Fine. He texted and asked if he should eat before he came out? (Oh for fuck's sake) I said I wouldn't be eating, but I didn't mind what he did. He then got worked up about whether or not to eat.

He said he didn't want to eat in front of me if I wasn't eating. (Oh Jeez). At that point I just gave up, and told him to forget it. He desperately needed to grow a pair. I didn't need to be someone else's comfort blanket.

Stewart - 'Malteser Man' - another dating agency introduction that I never met up with. We spoke on the phone for about an hour. He worked for Maltesers, in product design, so I suggested the Malteser bar to him (yeah, you probably have me to thank for that!) He talked pretty much non stop about himself, his car, his plasma TV and his job. After his 45 minute monologue, he asked 'Is there anything else you'd like to know about me?' I said 'No'. He sounded put out. (In hindsight, I should have asked him if I could have a commission for coming up with the Malteser bar idea.)

Simon - There's nothing more off-putting than a man who feels it necessary to score himself out of 10 in the bedroom. He gave himself an 8. Personally I thought it was more like a minus 3.

That bastard parakeet is also due for a spell on the 'island' if he continues to taunt me. Latest parakeet news to follow in the next installment. (Far more interesting than my current love life) Just wish he hadn't disappointed me with this threesome thing. I mean, isn't one enough?

One would be enough for me, as I've finally got to the stage now, where I'm ready to try and find 'him' again....For no man (or woman) is an island.

BREADED CHICKEN THEORY

13/03/2014

....PARAKEET NEWS....

This morning the parakeet had been ousted from his perch by a fat wood pigeon, his 2 little friends were no longer there - he had clearly tired of them and he was in flight. Typical male. I have suggested speed dating to him, but he says it's for losers. Fair enough.

And so to Breaded Chicken Theory...

In the good old days, when I was younger and thinner, I actually managed to get more than a single date with a guy, and I would eventually invite them round for dinner. I had a special 'date menu' which, for the main course, usually consisted of breaded chicken - it wasn't too heavy, was quick to cook, didn't have too much garlic, and everyone loved it.

But every single time I cooked this dish for a date, the date would cancel, or just not show up at all, and I'd never hear from them again. And after this happened 4 or 5 times, I began to get the impression that something strange was going on. At first I thought it might be the Grim Reaper - stalking my dates and telling them that if they went on another date with me that it would be their last. But it never seemed to happen when I wasn't cooking that meal. The breaded chicken was silent on the matter - this was surely a sign of guilt. I suspected fowl play! And so the 'Breaded Chicken Theory' was born.

I haven't cooked for a date in 3 years. But if I ever do again, I will make sure it isn't breaded chicken. I wonder what breaded parakeet would taste like...
Here's how I think the dating timeline works:

1st date - Meet for drinks and enjoy each other's company
2nd date - Home-cooked dinner at mine, great conversation, a kiss to end the night
3rd date - Nice evening out, come in for coffee, maybe we end up in bed.
4th date - Who the hell am I kidding?

For the last 3 years I have shunned dating. Not because I didn't want a boyfriend - it would be really nice to have one again - but I absolutely couldn't stand going on another date with another guy that I didn't know. The disappointment was too much to bear (mostly their disappointment at seeing me.) The problem with dating complete strangers is that they only go by first impressions. They assume that I have nothing to give, because I'm not Angelina Jolie. But I have lots to offer, and if they had the time to get to know me better, like the people that I work with, they would see what kind of a person I am. This is why I have only ever had successful relationships with people I worked with, and I have no faith in internet dating or dating agency introductions. It's all about the physical.

These total strangers don't care that I cook like Nigella, or that over the last 3 years I've become really good at studio lighting, or the fact that I have had BBC Producers and Hollywood agents interested in my screenplays and novels. Never mind that if they gave me a chance they would see that I'm a lovely person, and not bad in bed! (If I do say so myself!) All these men seem to care about is what I'd look like hanging off their arm. If you don't look the part, you are cast aside. You are invisible.

Reading this you might think that I have a real downer about how I look, but I really don't, I'm just reacting to the way I've been treated and the comments I've had from men over the recent years. My self-esteem has plummeted to a point where I no longer believe that anyone would find me attractive, and when somebody acts like they do, I find it very hard to trust and talk myself out of doing anything about it.

My boyfriend Mike from Devon once said I had 'blubber' - he had quickly apologised for his comment, but I said 'It's Ok. I'm thick skinned,' and then added 'That'll be the blubber.'
But I've had crap like that from guys that I wasn't even on a date with.

A couple of years ago, when I was looking for new friends in my area, I found a website that was simply about finding friends, not dates. David from High Wycombe messaged me and asked if I'd like to go to the cinema with him. So, we arranged to go and see 'The Inbetweeners' movie. I arrived at the cinema and waited for him, and eventually he turned up. Yet again, another disappointed look, but we went into the cinema, and collected the tickets. I went off to the kiosk to grab a drink, and when I came back he had gone. Completely vanished.

I watched the movie on my own, and was glad I'd stuck around to see it. But what harm would it have done him to sit there and just watch it with me?

So when I think about going internet dating again, or speed dating, it fills me with absolute horror. I have to don my imaginary armour and pretend that none of it really matters. Treating somebody like shit does not make you better than them.

I don't care if these guys go home to their mates and call me every horrid name under the sun, but to hurt somebody to their face, when they have done nothing wrong is unacceptable.

I may use some of my dates as comedy fodder, but I would never want to hurt them in reality - which is why I use false names.

Luckily, you get used to the bad behaviour and eventually it just washes over you. I may have had my confidence dented, but at least I haven't lost my sense of humour. Thankfully it has seen me through the bad times, as have my best friends. These days, navigating the dating pool is difficult and dangerous, and you need every ounce of courage to continue on against all the odds.

Men like David are just chicken - I wonder what he'd taste like breaded!

I BUY LINGERIE THEN IT ENDS

16/03/2014

Sometimes I like to take songs and change the lyrics to match what I'm thinking or feeling, so here's a song for you...

I picked some fine men
(To the tune of 'Lucille' by Kenny Rogers)

Shaz had a mission, she'd made a decision
On her sofa she took off her ring
She'd had it with Will, but it took her until
She watched 'Four Weddings' on the TV
Will's passions were racing and stretcher-
chasing
He liked to referee basketball
Shaz said 'The wedding is cancelled, you're no
Nigel Mansell,
and I'm keeping the saucepans an' all'

[chorus]
I picked some fine men to be my boyfriend!
I'm fed up of dating, for true love I'm waiting
I buy lingerie, then it ends
I've had some bad guys and also some mad guys
When will I just find The One?
Can't stand the speed-dating, I'm done.

Thought Matt was a keeper, he could not have
been sweeter,
On their first date, kissed Sharon real nice,
A consultant in IT, drove a Masserati
He got her into his bed twice
But soon she began thinking, that he wasn't into
women
When he refused to sixty-nine
He kept chilled mascarpone, should have known
he was phoney
And he liked his interior design!

[Chorus]

Jake was a dear, but he did love his beer
Well, his passion was actually 'Real Ale'
Sharon felt snubbed, he said 'dessert's in the pub'
He was acting like a typical male
A meal couldn't have been worse, ruined by his
thirst
It was clear that he just didn't think
So Sharon decided that their love was one-sided
In the end all he cared for was drink.

[Chorus]

Niall and Scotty, they must have been dotty
They put Sharon's head in a mess
They both kept her waiting, with their hesitating
It caused Sharon nothing but stress
But Scott was caught cheating, Niall wasn't into
meeting

And it turns out that that's what you get
For all your trouble, the heartache is double
So don't date guys from t'internet.

RELATIONSHIPS ARE SIMPLE

19/03/2014

One of my male friends reckons relationships are simple. I don't know where he gets this idea from. If relationships were simple there would be no need for 'The Jeremy Kyle Show'. I rest my case.

Relationships are complex, far more complex than even Heisenberg's Uncertainty Principle.

My friend reckons the secret to successful relationships are the 'Three Cs' - Communication, Commitment and...something else beginning with a 'C', which I have forgotten. (I've just texted him) He now says he's changed it to the 'Five Cs' (the young are so fickle!) which are: Caring, Communication, Compromise, Commitment and Consideration. He's very wise for one so young. Maybe these 5 things combined are the perfect recipe for a successful relationship, but I have one other magic ingredient to add which doesn't begin with a 'C'.   Admiration.

I find that to really desire someone, to feel a connection with them, you have to admire something about them, and not just their looks.

People get older, looks fade and if you haven't got anything else to fall back on, what happens to the relationship then?

If you love the way someone looks, but hate their personality, what is the point in having a relationship with them? And don't tell me it's because of sex - some men have sex with cars, bread, sheep – and, mostly, those are not that good looking!
So it cannot just be about that. I think it's more about showing off to their peers. (My sheep is far more attractive than yours! Therefore I am a stud. Or I have a French Stick and all you have is a finger roll!) What it's really about is insecurity.

I know a man in his early forties, Declan, and he's been in a relationship with Anna, a much younger woman, for many years. Anna, it seems, is a bit of a handful and has been known to damage his car and glue his door locks in fits of jealousy. Declan admits that he is only with her because she is 'well fit'. Last year he asked her to marry him. She refused, as she said he was getting too old! But still he remains in a relationship with this woman. Why?!! He is clearly terribly insecure and has an irrational fear of being single.

But what's wrong with being single? I'll admit it can take a while to get used to after being in a relationship for so long - deciding which side of the bed to sleep on - in the middle works best. Getting full control of the Sky remote is always a winner. Cooking whatever you like, and not having to eat vegetarian all the time. Having the freedom to do what you want, when you want and with whom you want. What's so bad about that?

Some people become co-dependent and lose themselves entirely in a relationship. I know this because that was how I was, in my first couple of relationships. It's one of those things that nobody ever tells you. I felt like I didn't exist if I wasn't with my 'other half'. How could I justify my own existence, if I wasn't with the person that loved me? I could only see myself through my partner's eyes, and that's a dangerous way to be.

If a tree falls in a forest, and no one is there to hear it, does it make a sound? And if no one is around to witness my existence, do I count? Am I a valid human being? Or is my life for nothing because I'm single?

It's like saying that you and your own opinions don't count. Are you the type of person who has to like everything that your partner likes?

It takes a real sense of security in yourself to admit to hating something that your beloved has a passion for - like Skiing or Basketball, or (heaven forbid) Butterflies!

My advice for anyone who knows they are not really in love with their partner would be: don't waste your life. Never be afraid to be on your own, because it's by being alone that you'll eventually realise who you really are, and what you want out of life. (It's doubtful that it will involve butterflies, but if it does, I wish you the very best of luck. Each to their own.)

I've spent a great deal of time on my own, and I feel like I'm finally at a stage where I do know who I am, what I want, and also what I definitely don't want, but it took a very long time to get here.

My last boyfriend Nick was quite a lot younger than me (9 years difference) but he and I were together for about a year, before I got fed up with his temper tantrums, his ability to alienate just about everyone around him, and the fact that he'd bought me a socket set and adjustable spanner for my birthday (no joke!)

When I broke up with him, he threatened to throw himself under a train such was the depth of his so-called 'love' for me.

He stormed out of the house with just a bottle of tequila and his driving licence. I was worried sick. I didn't know what to do, but I knew I wasn't going to give in to any emotional blackmail from him. I phoned his mother, who was clearly used to this kind of behaviour and was able to calm me down.

Luckily he came back a few hours later, none the worse. Exactly two weeks after this incident, he told me he had fallen in love with someone else! One weekend just before he moved out, I was meant to be going camping in Wiltshire with friends, but I'd decided to come back early. When I arrived home, there was a strange car across my driveway, and this new woman of his was in my shower. Nick had slept with her in my house, only two weeks after threatening to kill himself over his love for me. Love is a fickle creature.

I may be a little older now, but I am not much wiser when it comes to love. One thing I do know for certain, however, is it's best to get out as quickly as possible, once you know that you're no longer in love and that ship has sailed.

'But, Sharon', I hear you say, 'What's happening with you and this (totes amazeballs) guy that's been flirting with you?'

Well, dear reader, I have no idea....I still don't know if he likes me in that way, and I can't ask him. It's a really difficult one. I see him occasionally and I can't say anything to him, because I don't know if he knows that I like him too. And I don't know if he reads this or not, or if he's worked out that it's him I'm talking about. God, it's so complicated, isn't it? Maybe I am just being too subtle. He does have my mobile number now, so he is at liberty to ring or text if he wants to chat, or even invite himself over for a friendly dinner. (And I'd let him choose the menu!) I would so love to know what's going on.

I find myself shaking my head in disbelief at the situation I find myself in. I just want to give myself a good hard slap in the face, and shout 'Snap out of it!' I know the deck is stacked against me, but once someone has taken residence in your heart it is very hard to evict them, whatever the circumstances.

I feel like the Captain of a sinking ship! Is that land ahoy? Or another iceberg?

SHALLOW CENTRAL

20/03/2014

Last night I got an urgent text message from one of my friends, Scarlet. When I say 'urgent' I don't mean that she was being menaced by a giant man-eating bee and needed me to give support and advice on pest control. No. She wanted to make me aware that she had just joined 'Tinder' and she was currently being chatted up by 7 men at once.

She said 'Get on Tinder now!' So being the kind of inquisitive, adventurous soul that I am, and urgently needing some new comedy dating material, I did as I was asked and downloaded the app. Of course I was dying to be chatted up by 7 men at once. In fact, just one would have done.

It took a few minutes to get used to the concept of how it worked. Call me old fashioned, but I'm used to the kind of dating sites where you read someone's profile - their carefully chosen words of what they're like, what they do, what their favourite colour is, whether they like butterflies or not etc, and then you choose whether or not they sound like the kind of person that you'd like to meet. But not so on Tinder. It's actually pretty simple...it was Shallow Central.

Photo after photo of every registered man aged between 18 - 55 within an 84km radius suddenly appeared before me. With a simple choice: fancy or not fancy? Crikey. How would I know if I fancied them just from a photo? It takes a lot more than that for me. But hell, I'm up for anything,

I found it really difficult, in all honesty, but I did manage to click 'like' for a few people. Within about 20 minutes I had a 'match' - someone I liked had 'liked' me too. (That'll make a nice change then!) His name was Gino, he was Italian, and 32 years old.

After asking me how I was and telling me that he was new to Tinder too, he wanted to know 'Are you close to Reading or far away from here?' I said I was in Buckinghamshire, so not a hundred miles away from him in Berks.

His next message was exactly what I had been expecting from the start (I have plenty of experience of internet chatting). He said '...don't want to be impolite...but what about an easy drink tonight?' (What the hell is an 'easy' drink?) Did an easy drink for him, mean a painful 40 mile drive for me? I must admit I did consider it for all of about 5 seconds - he was pretty cute. But no, it was late (well, 8:30pm!) I was really tired, I had my comfy trousers on (the ones with the elasticated waistband) I hadn't eaten, I'd had a bad day.

And I'd never had an 'easy' drink with a stranger in my life. They were all difficult drinks as far as I was concerned. I've never been totally comfortable with meeting someone for a blind date, and certainly wasn't in the mood for company last night. I'm not always the most spontaneous person, usually the only spontaneous thing I want to do is combust, especially when faced with men who just want to take advantage.

So I told him I had to be up early, and said I hoped he got lucky. He innocently said 'About what?' (I guessed the full meaning of this was a little lost in translation to him.) But he told me to let him know in the future if I would be up for a drink - say tomorrow. I told him I'd let him know.

There was a time when, in my late twenties, I was really quite up for meeting men on the internet, but after finding it mainly populated with liars and fantasists, I gave it up as a bad job. I just couldn't make myself do it any more. It was emotionally painful. And men were constantly trying to have cybersex with me. I personally think cybersex is like the Diet Coke of sex. Absolutely pointless. I much prefer The Real Thing, (In Coke and sex.)

I remember one evening being particularly bored and faking participation, letting some bloke tell me exactly what he wanted to do to me. Faking it on the internet is really pretty easy, unless, of course, you're on Skype. You just keep your finger on the 'M' key. 'mmmmmmmmm'. Like that. Really gets 'em going! He was really getting into it, and every time he typed anything, I just hit the 'm' key a few times. Sometime during the 'conversation' I got up to make myself a coffee. He just kept going. When I got back with my drink I gave it a few more 'm's to make up for being absent. He seemed to like that. He typed 'You seem to be enjoying yourself. Where are your hands?' So I told him. They were on a biscuit. I couldn't lie. Cybersex just does nothing for me. Phone sex on the other hand... that's a whole different ball game (if you'll pardon the pun.)

A good few years ago, I was happily internet chatting to two men at once. I am a multi-tasker, after all! (let's call them 'TK-421' and 'Red5') (Yes, I am a Star Wars fan) when suddenly they both decided they wanted to try and coax me into cybersex at the same time! I only had the one 'm' key! What the hell was I to do? I really wasn't interested anyway, so I came up with a way of keeping them both happy. 'A plan so cunning, you could put a tail on it and call it a weasel!' in the words of Edmund Blackadder.

I told 'TK-421' that I was going to have to log off and sign in with an alternate screen name, as I was being bothered by an online pest. I told him that my alternate screen name was 'Red5'.

To 'Red5' I told exactly the same story, but that my new screen name was 'TK-421'. I then sat back, giggled to myself, and waited. I actually had to wait longer than I thought, before I heard back from either of them.
It had taken them a good 20 minutes to work out they were both men, having cybersex with each other! But at least they seemed to have a sense of humour about it. How I would have loved to have been a fly on the wall for that conversation. Evil? Me?

This morning I coined a new word, 'T'intercourse' - meaning sex you have with someone you meet on the internet. See if we can get that one into the Urban Dictionary, shall we?

THANK YOU FOR THE MUSIC

23/03/2014

When we decide to leave a relationship (or we get booted out of one) there are certain things we take with us - apart from the emotional pain and crushing heartbreak, of course. I'm talking about the inherited things - new tastes in music, food, leisure activities. New things we've tried and loved (like Thai food), or things we've learned to hate (like basketball.) There's also the knowledge that we acquire from a partner, like rules of sports, motor racing tips (keep to the racing line), what a socket set is used for, and useful things like that.

My last boyfriend used to smoke around me a lot, and he left me with something not so nice - asthma.

Call them the 'spoils of love' - love them or hate them, there's no getting away from them. As much as I want to try and forget some of the things that my past relationships have left me with, some memories are brought back with absolute clarity when I see, or hear, or smell something familiar.

With the smell of 'Joop', I'm 26 again, and madly in love with Jack, my most favourite boyfriend. He kept a journal. So I started a journal. And thank goodness I did, or else I might have forgotten some of the funniest dating experiences I ever had. He introduced me to the band 'Garbage' and I've loved them ever since. Thankfully he and I are still good friends, so that's something else I can take away from that relationship.

Every time I see a helicopter, or try and watch 'The Shawshank Redemption', I am reminded of Fred and his bizarre idea of how to seduce a woman.

I drive past the sign for Marwell Zoo, and have to stop myself laughing.(As do some of my friends, I'm told.) 'Have you ever been to Marwell Zoo?'

I see a socket set and I want to throw it at somebody. And then I wonder what the hell happened to my adjustable wrench.

But I wonder what they've taken from their time with me... I have no idea. I'm not sure I asserted my ideas on them enough to have left them with very much at all, sadly. Although one of them did remind me the other week that on one of our dates he had to help me get a bath tub up the stairs.

So that's a new learned skill, isn't it? Not a complete waste of time. At least he didn't have to deal with the solid oak wardrobe! I nearly killed myself trying to get that up the stairs.

Totally unrelated to the subject of this post - my friend Scarlet has just phoned me up to tell me something that she wants me to share on here, and to be honest this is fecking hilarious... so I will share it.

She met a guy called Andy while working on a project with him years ago. Andy has fancied her for ages (well actually since she lost a lot of weight) but he's been engaged to another woman, so Scarlet refuses, quite rightly, to get involved with him. Last year he came to stay at her house, and tried it on with her, but again she refused him and he cried on the phone to her when she said she was going to tell his fiancée. Anyway, he got back in contact with her this week and told her the wedding was off, and asked her if she'd consider dating him. She ignored the kind offer, and said she was sorry to hear about it.
This evening he phoned her to tell her that actually the wedding was still on, and being a big Star Wars fan he'd set it for May the 4th... (Read it again) (Terrible) (But absolutely true.)

But...and here's the best bit, he's told my friend that he will call off the wedding if she agrees to go out with him. She is gobsmacked to say the least. She is also wondering why she is always the consolation prize to unavailable men. She's apparently had 3 offers in the last 24 hours (lucky girl!) That's at least 2 more than me.

After Scarlet just told me her tales of woe, I asked her about what she's taken away from past relationships, but the only thing that sprung to her mind was the fear of men with giant heads. Her last boyfriend had an abnormally large head - so large in fact that it had its own gravitational pull.

It was like the Death Star apparently. Bringing us nicely back to Star Wars. If only Obi Wan had had a lisp...May the 4th be with you! Brilliant.

THE THRILL OF THE CHASE

24/03/2014

It's not very often I sit at my computer with a blank screen in front of me, at least not for very long. I usually have something to say, but today I have completely blanked on ideas for this blog. Even though I am currently being chatted up on Tinder (by 3 men at the same time).

One of them (Darren, 47) (old enough to know better) wanted to know if I'd ever been put across a man's knee (!!) I lied and said 'Never. What's it like?' (What I meant was what was it like for him being put across a man's knee, but I doubt he got the subtle inference.) Then he replied, going into the finer detail of what it was all about and saying that he wanted to spank me! I know I can be a little mischievous at times, but that's taking the punishment a little far, especially as he's never met me (and now never likely to either.) That's more like post 4th date behaviour, or have I just been out of the loop too long?

The other 2 conversations were far tamer in comparison. Gerald (33) from Chester is already preparing for our second date, even though we haven't actually met yet.

I told him if we got along I would cook dinner for him. He has specified Thai food, which is luckily also my favourite and my speciality. I doubt we will ever actually meet though. I am a realist. And Chester's a long way. And screaming the name 'Gerald' in bed really doesn't work for me.

I'm not looking at any of these men as a viable proposition. Why not? These men are far too easy. Personally I like more of a challenge. I'm a classic Gemini, a girl who enjoys the thrill of the chase. If a guy makes it too easy for me, I lose interest or run in the opposite direction at a hundred miles an hour. I like there to be a little give and take in the pursuit of love. The teasing, the flirting, the wondering if the other person likes you or not, it's all part of the game. That's the exciting part. Once you've been given free reign with their heart, it's game over, and on to the serious business of a relationship. Or not, as the case may be.

I once dated someone called Rob - he was a little younger than me and was totally into me, of that he left me no doubt. I liked him well enough, we had a laugh, but I wasn't really sure he was long-term relationship material. He just didn't interest me enough. There was no mystery there, and there was nothing about him I really admired.

One weekend, I planned a romantic getaway to Canterbury (I know, Canterbury isn't quite Venice, but I was on a budget, and Venice is for the really special ones!) In the hotel room with the 4-poster bed, he opened his suitcase - what was I expecting? Maybe some champagne, a bumper pack of condoms, perhaps even a silk scarf or pair of handcuffs - but no, none of the above, instead he pulled out his teddy bear!

Now, having a teddy bear is all well and good, but did I want it coming on a romantic weekend with the two of us? No I did not. He had my full attention in bed, so what the hell was the bear for? It wasn't even a particularly nice looking bear, it was knitted for one thing, and had buttons for eyes, and looked like something his Gran might have knitted for him. It was Mr Bean's teddy bear, and so he proceeded to do his Mr Bean impersonation. Talk about taking the romance out of a situation in one fell swoop. I stopped seeing him soon after that. I wouldn't be surprised if he still had that bear.
Men who need comfort blankets are not for me. I'm quite adventurous myself (at least when it comes to travel, food and dating) and I'm looking for someone who is, at least, the hero of his own life story, and not someone who thinks Mr Bean is the height of comedy, or that butterflies are cool.

I don't like to be smothered by love. I like a guy to back off once in a while and keep me interested. I don't want someone who's around 24/7. Does that make me weird? Or is that what everyone wants in an ideal world? I like a guy to let me know he's interested, of course, but once I've been made aware, I expect to do my fair share of the running. I love organising romantic dates, meals, and weekends away - I don't necessarily expect him to be romantic, he is a man after all, but it would be nice if he appreciated the gesture. Best tip to any man wanting to impress a woman is not to buy her a socket set or an adjustable spanner, or in fact, any DIY equipment, unless she has specified that that is what she wants.

So with whom have I had this fabled 'Thrill of the Chase' - well with quite a few men actually, especially the ones I've worked with. There's always that 'Should I, Shouldn't I? dilemma with people you work with, which adds a bit of extra excitement, but I find those are the people that I get to know the best, and therefore have the greatest admiration for. They also tend to like me for me, which is always a bonus. If they can really make me laugh then they're already half way to my heart.

A FETE WORSE THAN DEATH?

25/03/2014

A couple of years back, my sister and her husband actually managed to set me up with someone I hadn't already dated, Dan. This was a turn-up for the books. Dan was also one of my brother-in-law's karate mates, but it turns out he and I had something in common - we both worked in the TV industry.

Dan worked for a broadcast hire company, a company I'd actually had dealings with. Great. We'd have something to talk about at least. The worrying thing was that my (at the time) 10-year-old niece had already nicknamed him 'Little Dan', and she was only about 4'6", so exactly how 'little' was he? My sister allayed my concerns by saying that he wasn't that tiny. Good. Not that tiny. But how tiny exactly?

Dan and I arranged to meet for drinks. We were both quite nervous, but we got along reasonably well. He was pretty short, but at least a couple of inches taller than me. He wasn't my usual type, but he was perfectly pleasant.

I let him talk about karate for most of the evening, which allowed him to get into his comfort zone. I don't remember much of what he asked me, or what else we talked about, but we did agree to meet up again.

On our second date he totally surprised me by suggesting going to a local fete. There were rides! I love rides. Brilliant! Couldn't have chosen a better date myself, apart from Thorpe Park. We had a great time, I even won a teddy bear (kill me!) on a shooting game. (I could totally have been an assassin in another life.) I must say my aim has improved dramatically since I started imagining the face of one of my difficult colleagues on the targets.

After going on the rides and marvelling at the 'Wall of Death', we walked a short distance to the local pub and had a couple of drinks. We got chatting about some of my interests. Apart from being interested in the inter-departmental warfare at work, I'm also into the paranormal, science, the nature of the universe in general, and also conspiracy theories. So we talked about these for a while too. But I fucked up and totally scared him off. Makes a nice change for me to be the one to screw up a perfectly good date. It does happen. Like the time I went all Kevin-Costner-in-The-Bodyguard on an insanely irritating wasp, spearing it on the dinner table with a steak knife.

___

I don't think my date was impressed. But I was. In fact I would have paid to see the action replay. Borrowing a phrase from my younger colleagues, it was 'like totally the coolest thing'!

There was an upside to my failure with Dan, of course - at least I didn't have to live with being teased by my nieces for the next several hundred years. I can still hear their taunts 'Shazzy loves Little Dan...Shazzy loves Little Dan' as both of them scream it repeatedly across the neighbourhood for all to hear. Thanks. And that's 'Auntie Shazzy' to you, you little terrors!

Yes, even my nieces make fun of my love life. Last month it was 'Shazzy's got a date with Derek' (not his real name) Derek is my best gay friend. How to explain that to (now) 10 and 12 year olds - actually they probably know more about it than me. One day, in the not too distant future, when they are dating, I shall get my own back.

I seriously doubt that I am ever going to find a man who really loves me for me, my flaws and all.

On these dating sites that I've joined (for research purposes only, of course) the guys don't ask me about what I like, or about my writing, or my job, they ask me about my cup size, what I'm wearing, whether I like feet... It's totally depressing. I don't know why I bother, but then I remember this blog, and the constant need for new material.

Occasionally when chatting to some of these guys, I might get to talk about cooking. What would I cook for them if they came to dinner at my house?... I tell them, and then they say if I cooked the perfect meal for them that they wouldn't be able to wait until the 3rd date to take me to bed. Not what I want to hear. What I want to hear is, 'I'm prepared to wait for you until you decide the time is right.' 'I want to be with you because you make me laugh.' 'I want to get inside your head, not just inside your pants.' But what I'm actually hearing is 'any port in a storm.'

I was always told that the way to a man's heart was through his stomach. This is a total falsehood. I still haven't figured out the way to a man's heart, but it is most definitely not through his stomach. If this were true, I would have men queuing round the block! Though I have found the way to anything below the waistline no great mystery. Show up.

Men are always wondering 'What do women want?' - well I'm going to clear this up once and for all, and tell you exactly what they want, right here, right now...

We have absolutely no fucking idea. (At least, no set idea.)
But I can tell you what we don't want. We don't want a guy to assume that we are easy, that our opinions don't matter, or that we are stupid. (If I want to feel stupid, I can listen to my clever colleagues talking about video codecs. That always does it for me.) We want a guy who will listen to us, not just hear what we say, but really take it in, and want to understand how our minds work. We want a guy to want to get to know us before trying to get us into the sack. Our opinions of you can be moulded, gentlemen. They are not set in stone. You ever seen the film 'Hitch'? Well, it's exactly like that. You have to make us girls believe that we could have a good relationship with you. Even the most stubborn woman's head can be turned by someone who seems really interested in more than just her bra size. Pay attention! Look me in the eyes!

For the special people that 'get' this, the checklist goes right out the window. There are worse fates, than ending up with someone who really cares about you and isn't afraid to show it.

That is the big secret. Use it to your advantage.

RED HOT DATE

27/03/2014

Earlier this evening a couple of my lovely 3rd year students interviewed me for their dissertations. The subjects were comedy, and people who make up fantasy online presences. I admitted to them that I had on occasion made up lies about myself online to disguise my true identity - mostly just about my job - there aren't many TV studio managers called Sharon - so I tend to tell the casual chatters that I am either 'a lingerie model', 'a fighter pilot' or 'Professor Brian Cox.' (Perhaps the latter is more believable than the lingerie model.)

Speaking of online presences, as I write this, my friend Scarlet is out on a date with someone she met on Tinder. She has had 4 offers this week, and most of those were actually from people she knows and not from online acquaintances. (Of course I am thinking 'Why the hell haven't I had 4 offers this week?') (Well???) (Bloody cheek!) So who is Scarlet's lucky gentleman? Well, I don't know too much about him, but I know they've had some pretty interesting conversations this week (mostly involving snorkels, from what I can ascertain) although surprisingly enough they've never spoken on the phone.

Now I personally would never meet a guy without first speaking to him on the phone - you tend to learn these things the hard way - like the time I had a date with someone who sounded like Joe Pasquale's slightly less masculine mate. (If you don't know what Joe Pasquale sounds like, YouTube him.)

I did warn Scarlet about the possibility that he might sound like Joe Pasquale - she hadn't considered that outcome, but after I mentioned it she wished she had spoken to him before arranging to meet. The deed was done.
There was no phoning him up, listening to his voice and then cancelling on him. What would she have told him? I'm sorry I can't meet you - you sound like a toddler on helium! Scarlet has no filter, so she probably would have said that to him.

But apparently, the date is going well - she's just texted me. There was a big debate last night about whether or not she found him attractive. His online profile had only showed one photo - a profile view with him holding a guitar - Scarlet likes guitarists, so she clicked 'Yes'.
After chatting to him for a few days and deciding she liked the things he said, she Facebook stalked him (Yes, fellas, we do that too!)

She wasn't keen on the photos she found though and was considering calling off their date, until I told her one of the secrets of photography - some people are just not photogenic, but it doesn't mean they're not attractive in person. (This also works in reverse, as I can testify - ie. you can make a pig's ear look like a silk purse) I told her she had to give him a chance. So she agreed.

She said she was only going to stay until 8:30pm - of course she had the stand-by story all ready - 'not staying too long, got an early start tomorrow' - the thing we always tell our dates when we don't know if we will get along with them or not. (Unless of course you are '2 Hour Man' and you always give your dates exactly 2 hours of your time, whether you like them or not!) She also had the emergency code word ready to text me in case she needed a get-out phone call. (I'm giving away all the secrets here.)

Anyway it's now 9:15pm, and I'm guessing she's still on the date, as she hasn't texted back yet, and I know she will. She will want to tell me every detail. Excellent. I look forward to it. She better not stay out 'til midnight though, because I will not be happy getting that phone call while I am dreaming of Gerard Butler, a tub of Haagen Dazs Pralines and Cream and a large spoon.

I actually deleted the Tinder app last night after becoming once more disillusioned with the whole online dating experience. The last message I received was 'I'm just after casual sex - Watford.' Great, if casual sex in Watford was what I was after (it wasn't...but how about [town where I live]?) It seemed like every man on there was after the same thing. And I think by 'casual sex' they mean one-time sex and then on-to-the-next-one. The kind of casual relationship I'm after, doesn't involve one night stands. I'd like something a bit more dependable - but maybe that isn't what 'casual' is. Maybe my version of casual is someone else's version of a committed relationship.

Desperate for new material, this calls for something radical... think I'll go out clubbing soon.

YOU HAD ME AT SHALLOW

28/03/2014

Last night, my friend Scarlet had a date with Jim - the bloke she met on Tinder. All seemed to be going quite well, she said, until they started discussing Tinder. Here's the gist of the conversation:

Jim: 'Tinder's the greatest application in the world!'
(Clearly this man is delusional - everybody knows that the best app is Tesco online.)
Scarlet: 'I wouldn't go that far.'
Jim: 'It's brilliant, and it enables me to be as shallow as I like and just pick the people I'm attracted to. I've got more dates arranged...'

And thus Jim lost himself a second date with my good friend. By admitting he was shallow and telling Scarlet that he had dates lined-up well into the next century, he proved himself to be a bad bet. Who would want to consider dating a man like that? Why could he not be satisfied with dating one woman at a time and seeing where it took him? Men like that are greedy, and there are plenty of them out there, especially on internet dating sites.

Scarlet says it made her feel really bad about herself, and I must admit I know exactly what she means. Why have I avoided dating for the last 3 years? Because men like that make us feel dispensable, irrelevant, replaceable. We are made to feel like ring doughnuts - just an object with a hole.

Maybe the age of romance really is dead. Where are all the nice guys? Is it a pipe dream to want to find someone normal and loving? In an age where ready meals have taken over from traditional cooking, it seems the only kind of love you can get is the fast kind. Quick, temporary, tasteless, and banal.

A couple of months ago, I got a surprise phone call. It was from a mobile number I didn't recognise. I stupidly answered it. It was some bloke I apparently used to chat to online many, many years ago. I didn't even remember him. Why the hell had he just decided to call me up out of the blue? We'd never even met. I was pretty dismissive of him on the phone, and answered his questions in a tone that clearly suggested it was none of his business - I really don't like getting calls from people who have no business calling me, especially from guys clearly just after casual relationships.

I very almost told him to piss off, but I didn't, because I am a lady, and I refuse to bring myself down to their level. There are times when I really wish I wasn't such a nice person and could actually tell someone exactly what I think of them.

This reminds me of something else that happened to me about 10 years ago, while I was still living in my haunted cottage. I'd been casually seeing Toby. The only thing that really interested me about Toby was the fact that he said he was psychic, could read people auras and told me all about the ghostly presences in my house. (Apparently there were 4 of them!) (Holy fuck!) (And they weren't even paying rent.)

Anyway, Toby wasn't the guy for me. I couldn't get over the goatee beard for one thing, or the resemblance to Adam Sandler. We didn't see each other after we'd had about 3 dates. But one night, several months later, around 2 am I got a phone call from Toby. He was clearly drunk and was with a male friend. He asked me (no word of a lie) if he and he mate could come over for sex. Both of them! At 2 am! (Heavy sigh, Sharon rolls her eyes.) Of course I said no, and went back to sleep, wishing for a special place reserved in hell for men with stupid goatee beards.

It's amazing the feeling of being brought right down to earth when you realise you're just a number in someone's little black book.

Some people are just lucky I guess. Some people manage to find partners that aren't just after sex. I hope they realise how lucky they are. In a world where you can shop for dates as easily as you can shop for milk, how do you know what's real love and what isn't? Where is the line between love and lust? Does love even exist anymore?

More speculation and rhetorical questions in the next instalment...

THE SPARK

05/04/2014

I've recently been chatting (via Whatsapp) (Yeah, I know, I'm so 'down with the kids'!) to a guy I met on an online dating site, Kieran. In text, he seems perfectly nice and normal, he said he thought I had some 'very attractive qualities' (always a bonus) and as we've been text chatting for a few days with no outward signs of him being a fuckwit, when he asked if he could phone, I said Ok.

So Kieran rang me, and I immediately regretted my decision, because although he sounds Ok by text, on the phone he sounded negative and depressing. He didn't have a good word to say about anything - and I'm much more of an optimist. He told me all about having to renovate his flat for sale, as he didn't get on with his neighbours (apparently they were 'arseholes') then went into the legalities of having wooden floors in an upstairs flat. He told me about his job working for London Underground, and how he never seems to get time to do the things he wants. Throughout our hour-long conversation, he talked and talked, I barely got a word in - when I did get a word in, he talked over me (I hate that.)

There was no laughter - and I'm always laughing - he seemed to have no sense of humour. Also he only asked me 2 questions during the whole hour he talked at me. The first was 'You don't work at the University of ****** do you?' Apparently in 1995 he had attended the university I work for - he'd been a film critic in an earlier job and had studied cinema and film. The 2nd question was 'How many bedrooms does your house have?' Not sure how this was relevant, unless of course he was planning to move in. By around 10 seconds into our conversation I had already decided that Kieran wasn't for me. For not only did he remind me of Marvin the Paranoid Android, but there was just no spark.

But what do I mean by 'spark'? Magnetism? Attraction? Electricity? Have you ever felt electricity? I don't mean like by sticking your fingers in an electrical socket, or licking a battery! In my job, I deal quite a bit with electricity and electrical safety (and students licking batteries!)

But the type of spark I'm talking about is what happens when the electricity you're dealing with isn't coming out of a wall socket. I hadn't really ever felt the physical sensation of a romantic spark until a few months ago.

It was the strangest feeling. A sudden sense that the air in the room was electrified - filled with static charge - and that in that atmosphere, something magic was happening. Like the electricity was something tangible.

What are you supposed to do when you feel a flow of electricity coming from a surprising other person? There are no electrical safety rules for that (believe me, I checked.) So how do you protect yourself? Rubber-soled shoes or lightning rods aren't going to help you. It's as if your whole body were full of iron filings, and you feel a kind of pull. You are helpless to its effects.

How was I to know if this electricity I was feeling was real or imaginary? There was no instrument to measure it. I couldn't put a voltmeter between us.

So instead, over the space of a few weeks, I watched and listened and tried to trust my instincts. (Anyone who knows me well enough will laugh at me now, because they know I always question my own instincts, analyse the minutiae of any situation and always find myself wanting.)

At one point during this period, the man in question gave me a perfect excuse to get right up close to him. I got right into his personal space, barely millimetres between us, and neither of us seemed in any hurry to move away. I must admit it wasn't something I would usually do, but I was testing the water.

And perhaps he was trying to engineer the physical proximity too. Who knows? There was a lot of accidental hand touching too, which would send my pulse into overdrive, but I didn't know if this was really accidental or not. It is a little bit of a mystery.

But that is what I mean by a spark. And not sure I'm going to find that with online dating.

I spoke to my friend Scarlet last night about my recent misadventures with internet dating sites and she said to me 'Why are you on *******? (crap online dating agency) and I said 'How else do I get priceless comedy material?' Anyway, I have some dates lined up soon.

Am I expecting a spark from them? Doubtful.

TWO SIDES OF THE COIN

07/04/2014

This week Scarlet and I both have dates. This may well be a first for us. Although Scarlet has had other dates recently, this will be my first date in a couple of years. As previously mentioned on here, I gave up dating for a long time because I'd got to the stage where I just couldn't stand going on any more dates with any more strangers. It had become too taxing for me - I had grown tired of pretending like I cared about their tastes in horror films, or their dislike of anything containing ginger. I just couldn't fake the smile any longer.

One of the last men I dated was Brian - what did we have in common? He liked cooking and he had two Yorkshire terriers - a male and a female. (I have one Yorkie, and he is more than enough trouble!) We met up for a walk near to where I lived, and we brought our dogs.

What started to put me off Brian? Well, for starters, he had the boy dog on a pastel blue lead and the girl dog on a pastel pink lead. (I have no words for this.) (I wanted to ask him if he had a tub of mascarpone waiting for him at home, but I resisted the temptation.)

Secondly, when we started talking about cooking, he got his phone out and started showing me photo after photo of all the food he'd recently cooked. I was underwhelmed by the whole experience. And the fact that he left me with wet jeans (no, not in that way!) he'd dragged me cross country on this 'special short cut' he knew, a mile through soaking wet, long grass, which both myself and my little dog had trouble wading through. He didn't get the second date he was after.

Anyway, recently I got the urge to start dating again - as U2 say 'Sometimes you can't make it on your own'. And once somebody 'jump starts' your heart it's very hard to put it back into storage, and I have tried. Life is so much easier when you're not on a constant emotional rollercoaster ride.

Scarlet is lucky when it comes to dating, she knows people who actually have single male friends. She doesn't have to rely on browsing through online sites, wondering who is telling the truth and who is not - wondering which ones are really married, or which ones might be foot fetishists etc etc. Her good friends actually set her up with single, available men with nice personalities. She doesn't have to pimp herself out - her friends will do it on her behalf.

She knows that when she turns up on that date, that the man she meets will have already been vetted by someone she knows, and that can only be a good thing.

Most of the men I have met have been a let down, to say the least. You just have to read the rest of this book to see that. But I have been on so many first dates that I have lost count, and so I am fairly immune to the usual effects some people might feel. Scarlet, for example, is currently 'bricking it' in her own words. She is nervous because she thinks she might actually really like this one. She has invested time and emotion, something that I used to do in her position. So where Scarlet is a nervous wreck, I am cool as a cucumber. Sometimes you can repeat something so many times that it becomes like second nature. That is how dating is for me. Unless, of course, I'm being offered a date with someone I really like - but that hasn't happened to me in a very, very long time.

The neural pathways are set. I am already expecting disappointment in one way or another, but this is how I have learned to protect myself. I always say 'If you expect disappointment, then you'll never be disappointed.'
So wish me luck, dear reader. Once more unto the breach....

THE RULES OF ENGAGEMENT

08/04/2014

This week my friend Scarlet has been texting me for advice. Yes, of course dating advice, what else? What do you mean I'm in no position to give advice about that? I'm the bloody dating expert. (Shut up!) Just because I happen to be single at the moment, don't think for one moment that I don't know what I'm talking about. Thank you. (If you can't take this seriously, then go and watch 'Game of Thrones' instead.)
So Scarlet's been chatting to someone new, and her texts have been something along the lines of:

'When should I text?'
'What should I text?'
'Why isn't he answering me?'
'I hate men, I hate men, I hate men'
And 'How long should I leave it before texting again?'

Isn't dating complicated? And this is before they've even met. Just wait until the sex part. (I'm so looking forward to those texts. Not.)
What Scarlet is beginning to realise, is that Dating is like Chess - it is a game with its own complex rules. When I say 'rules' of course, I don't mean actual rules, they're more like 'guidelines'.

These guidelines are not written down anywhere, although knowing the blogosphere, someone, somewhere will have had a try (but now it's my turn.)   These are guidelines that are learned, usually by bitter experience, there are no books for this sort of thing - although some so-called 'self help' books go some way to try to clear up the mysteries of dating, but they are far too preachy for my liking. I am a realist, and I understand human frailty, especially when it comes to dating. So you can throw 'The Rules' out the window for now, because...

...here are my personal guidelines for the dating 'game'...

1. Stay single. Hahaha!   No, but seriously.

2. If you have your mind set on dating, try not to become obsessed with the object of your desire. How do you know if you're obsessed? Are you reading his horoscope? Are you constantly thinking about what he's doing? Are you stalking him on Facebook? Have you made up an iTunes playlist with music that reminds you of him? Do you think about hyphenating your two surnames together for after the wedding? Have you picked out curtains? If the answer to any of these questions is 'yes', then you are obsessed. (Return to point 1 immediately, for your own sanity.)

3. If you do find yourself becoming obsessed, don't text him too often. If, late at night, or slightly drunk, you suddenly get the urge to text him yet again, either get a friend to confiscate your phone, try thinking about Benedict Cumberbatch / Hugh Laurie / or whoever floats your boat, go and watch 'Game of Thrones', or eat a tub of Ben & Jerry's finest.

4. If you have ignored point 3, and have actually late-night texted him, do not wait around for a reply. Do not text your friend (who will no doubt be in bed, asleep, dreaming of Gerard Butler) and ask her why he hasn't replied yet. (She will not know either, but will kindly suggest that he's either asleep, out with his mates, has lost his phone, or is dead.) Do not lose faith and say that you'll cancel the date with him if he doesn't reply. Just wait it out, be a man.

5. Do not 'like' his every post on Facebook. Limit yourself. One 'like' per week is plenty. Do not share his every status. Do not go through his photos tagging everyone you know in them. Do not send a self-congratulatory text to your friend every time he 'likes' your post.

6. Do not assume he is Facebook stalking you. Just because he happens to come online a couple of minutes after you've posted your latest status about finding a weirdly shaped vegetable in your fridge, does not mean that he is obsessed with you too.

7. If he really is Facebook stalking you, this is no reason to call the police. (Go back to point 1 if you start feeling this way.)You should be flattered.

8. Do not, ever, EVER, admit to him how you feel about him. Not until you are safely married and there is no easy escape. Of course, if he tells you he loves you first, then it's ok, but then and only then. Do not allude to it, do not hint, do not offer to bare his children at every opportunity. Do not write him love poetry, ever.

9. If he really isn't interested in you, give up. Do not spend years and years wasting your time and emotion on someone who clearly is just blindly obsessed with the very pretty Susan, from the Human Resources department, who has the personality of a haddock - completely lacking in wit, intelligence and sense of humour.

10. If you're lucky enough to get asked on a date by the one you desire, do not mess it up by doing any of the following things: Do not arrive drunk / wearing slippers. Do not talk all night about the terrible time you've had with your ex. Do not moan about your job / life / diet. Do not pretend to like the things he likes - one day when you're married, he will find you out. Do not fall over and flash your control underwear. Do not bring your knitting along for when the chat runs dry.

11. Assuming the first date has gone well, you may leave him with a kiss. (On the lips, or the cheek - nowhere below the neck.) Do not take him back to your place, unless he is driving you there.
Do not invite him in for 'coffee'. You may text him and tell him that you had a lovely evening. You should at no point log on to Facebook and update your status as 'I love him, I love him, I love him.'

12. The second date is the real test of whether or not you're still both interested in each other. Is there still a spark? Is the conversation flowing, or has he reverted to showing you photographs of all the food he's cooked recently? Has he asked you if you've ever been to Marwell Zoo? (If he has, run away now, while you still can.) But if things are still going well, then you can suggest a third date.

13. The third date is when he'll most likely be expecting to get you naked. (At least he will if he's been reading this.) Hopefully you won't suddenly find out that he has a surprise foot fetish, or that he likes to wear a nappy and be spanked. (These things should have already been mentioned during the texting period between dates 2 and 3.) (If he has sprung a bizarre taste in sexual practices on you, get him out of the door as fast as possible and revert to point 1.) If his tastes seem relatively normal, just go with it and enjoy.

14. If he's still in contact with you after the 3rd date, then you're well on your way to an actual relationship. Well done. Now, go away, because I hate you! Just kidding. But do try not to text your single friends about it constantly, telling them how wonderful everything is, as they are likely to disown you.

15. If the third date doesn't go so well, revert to the last 3 suggestions of point 3. Then, when you're ready to try again, get back on that horse, and don't let the failures keep you down.
Ok, so not exactly 'The Rules' but a good start I reckon, and certainly more useful than 'If he phones you on Thursday to ask you out for the Saturday, tell him you're busy.' Crap. If he does take the time to phone you on a Thursday to ask you out on Saturday, say 'Yes please,' or else some other lucky girl may snap him up.

_____

I know I would.

THE SEVEN DEADLY SINS OF DATING

10/04/2014

We've all heard of the 'Seven Deadly Sins' of the Christian tradition - Lust, Gluttony, Greed, Sloth, Wrath, Envy and Pride. They are described as being 'Transgressions fatal to spiritual progress'. (Yes, I Googled it.) So what about the Seven Deadly Sins of Dating? What are they? (Transgressions fatal to marital progress?) How can we avoid falling for their folly, and risking the eternal dating damnation of being placed in partnerless purgatory? (That's a triple point score for alliteration.)

Following on from the last chapter, I thought I'd share some of the insights into why some dates end in disaster - well, some of my dates, anyway. These are some of the classic mistakes that play a part in the date's demise - some of which have been my own fault, but most were not down to me or my errors in judgement. Some dates I can only admit to having purposefully sabotaged so that I wouldn't have to text them later with 'Sorry, but I didn't feel that there was any chemistry.'

1. Desperation

When you are faced with someone reeking of desperation, there is nothing you can say or do to put them off. They are desperate for a relationship with anyone. Anyone at all. You can see that they don't really care about whom they date, they just need a companion, as they are usually too scared to do anything by themselves. Here are the signs: They don't ask anything about you. They talk over you. They make overly romantic gestures on a first date - like bringing roses and champagne. They don't listen to what you want, or what you have to say. They ignore the fact that you have nothing in common. Even though you dislike everything they like, they still want to meet you for a second date.

2. Depression

When the first thing that your date says to you is 'I don't know why I put myself through this', you know you're in for a long night. These are the complainers, the people who never see the bright side of anything. Is it any wonder why they are single? They are the people who never have a good word to say, who are always wondering why the universe has it in for them. Who would want to date a person like that? You want your 'other half' to brighten your day, not bring you down to earth with a bump.

They have high expectations that cannot ever possibly be fulfilled, and this makes the universe a very sad place for them. My advice: take a Prozac, try to be thankful for the good things, and remember there are people worse off than you – some of them like doing butterfly jigsaws.

3. Lust
Some people just can't help themselves, when it comes to sex. These people are commonly known as 'men' (I'm just kidding!) They are not content to wait until the third date to try and discover what you look like naked. Some men don't even make it to a first date because they use lines like 'What's your cup size?' and 'Are you shaved?' to try and size someone up. Women, in general, don't wish to be treated like sex objects. We want to be wooed by your words and won-over by your fabulous personality. We do not fall in love with you because you have an enormous cock, or because you might be great in bed. We do not care that you can make your penis twirl like the blades of a helicopter, or that you have balls the size of watermelons. On our first date with you we would like it very much if you could leave our breasts un-fondled. Telling a woman that you 'like to get to know a person by having sex with them first' will not win you a second date. Sometimes, however, you can use sex to get what you want, especially if what you want is to be left alone.

4. Arrogance

We know that you think you're great. But scoring yourself out of ten, in the bedroom, isn't going to win you any points with us, especially if you're really not that good. Instead of telling us about how you 'transfer large sums of money between London and Tokyo on a daily basis' why don't you ask us about ourselves and see what we think are admirable qualities that will win you a relationship. During a speed dating event, don't sit back in your chair and say that you're only there to boost the numbers. And don't tell us that you always spend exactly 2 hours with a date, whether you like them or not. In either case you will look like a prize dick, and people will write comedy blogs about you.

5. Emasculation

One for the ladies here... I have been told that men, in general, like to feel like they are the protectors, the rescuers, the ones who are needed, the dependable ones. Don't take this away from them by trying to behave like one of them. Demonstrating your ninja skills on an unsuspecting wasp, at the dinner table, isn't going to get you into his bed. Instead ask for his help with something, make him feel valued. But also, on the flip side, you'll never find a man dumbing himself down to be in relationship with a woman, so why should you do it?

Some men actually enjoy dating a woman who is intelligent and funny. So don't sell yourself short, ladies.

6. Rudeness

Being rude, or generally disagreeable is also a real no-no on a date. If a date asks you a perfectly valid question like 'Where did you learn to speak such good Spanish?' don't sarcastically answer 'Japan'.

Your date will probably have already got the message that you are not interested, by your one-word answers and from the disappointed look on your face when you entered the room. Being rude to them will make your date feel incredibly uncomfortable. If you really don't feel like you can face another second in his / her company, make your excuses and leave. Don't prolong their agony - they are also having to put up with you, and are wasting valuable energy faking a smile.

7. Lying

If you have told your date, previous to meeting, that you are 32 years old, 6'2" and with a full-head of hair, don't turn up and be 62, 3'2" and bald. On your dating profile try to include recent photos of yourself, not photos from 20 years ago, and not of Brad Pitt / Jason Statham / Angelina Jolie (delete as appropriate)

Don't tell your date that you're really into quantum physics and researching the birth of the universe, when you're really only interested in watching 'Made in Chelsea' on the telly and eating Cadbury's Creme Eggs in vast quantities. After the wedding you will be found out, and this will lead to bitterness, frustration and will be taken as possible grounds for divorce. Do tell your date about your real interests. Keeping a little bit of mystery is good and you can leave things out at this stage, especially if you are into weird sexual practices or photographing butterflies. You should always leave something to talk about on the second date.

So, those are my Seven Deadly Sins to avoid while on a date. (If you have any to add please feel free to write your own blog!)

By definition there can only be seven, and I have tried to pick the best ones. There are others like timekeeping and grooming, but I feel they are minor irritations compared with the choices above.
If you are thinking of taking someone on a date, try to learn from my experience and remember some of the dos and don'ts. And if you pride yourself on lusting after an envious sloth, you only have yourself to blame.

A WRETCHED HIVE OF SCUM AND VILLAINY

13/04/2014

I hadn't been out dancing or clubbing for a very long time, but on Friday night I finally got the chance for a proper night out in Watford, as my sister had invited me out with her friends. She had warned me about their regular haunt and had made it sound a bit like the Mos Eisley space port, for any of you Star Wars fans out there. "You will never find a more *wretched hive of scum and villainy*. We must be cautious." (That's Obi Wan Kenobi, not my sister.) My sister actually said something along the lines of 'It's a regular hang out for sex pests and perverts.' (Excellent. Send them my way.) So that was pretty much what I was expecting. And I wasn't disappointed.

I hadn't met my sister's friends before, but they were brilliant, and seemed up for a laugh, which was lucky because you couldn't help but laugh at the venue. It was clear as soon as we went in, that my sister knew pretty much everybody there, including the DJ. She introduced me to Bradley Cooper. Not THE Bradley Cooper, but someone they (for someone unknown reason) nicknamed 'Bradley Cooper.'

He didn't look anything like Bradley Cooper. He was in his early fifties for a start. My sister said he had 'Bradley's Cooper's body and the head of a Chuckle Brother.' Well, she wasn't far wrong about his head - although a bit better looking than a Chuckle Brother. The body thing I couldn't tell, but it didn't look too much like Bradley Cooper's to me - not that I've experienced it at close quarters.

My sister also pointed out the people to avoid. 'The Stalker' was one of them. I can't remember too much about what he looked like, but I think he was short, probably in his early fifties with white hair and glasses.
To be honest he did look like a bit of a sex pest, and he kept trying to chase my sister around the dance floor. This was pretty hilarious, though my sister didn't think so.

I don't really drink much when I'm out, I'd had a couple, but I was actually stone cold sober for the whole experience. My sister complained that I wouldn't be able to appreciate the 'atmosphere' of the place unless I was completely trollied. But she was wrong. I completely appreciated it. It was one of the funniest nights out I've had in ages. (Ok, so it was the only night out I've had in ages.)

While we were on the dance floor, my sister kept pointing out good looking men and asking me if I'd like to get to know them better. This was completely embarrassing, and I shyly hid my head in my hands and kept saying 'No,' to every man she pointed to. Eventually she ignored my protests, pointed at one who was stood near the bar, and actually beckoned him over to her. Yes, she beckoned him. I was impressed at her balls. I wouldn't have had the courage to do that, but maybe I just wasn't drunk enough. So he came over and she got chatting to him - I learned later that she was 'bigging me up' -telling him that I was a great cook. I don't know what else she told him, but he seemed up for a dance. Poor man. I wasn't sure if he was dancing with me because he liked the look of me, or because he felt bad for me. I didn't need the sympathy, I tried to avoid eye contact as much as possible.

But I asked him a bit about himself - Freddie was 39 years old and from Kosovo. His English was pretty good though, luckily, so I could just about understand what he was saying over the loud music.

So we danced for a bit, and then he left to go and get another drink. I breathed a sigh of relief. I wasn't sure I was ready to pick up a complete stranger.

But then after a few minutes he actually came back. Ok, so maybe he was interested, even if it was just in my cooking.

———

152

My sister's friends kept giving me the thumbs up sign and raising their eyebrows and eventually I got more comfortable in his company and decided to give him a chance. After an hour or so, he asked me to come and sit down and chat, so I did. He told me he worked as a manager in the construction industry and lived in Middlesex. He asked me about my job and where I was from and all the usual questions, then he asked if I was busy on Saturday and would I like to go on a date. I was quite taken aback, but I said yes. He seemed like a nice enough guy.

We carried on dancing together and I was trying out my salsa moves, to a bit of Gloria Estefan, but I don't think he'd ever taken any salsa lessons, so they were lost on him. We had a great time and at the end of the evening my sister was trying to convince him that he wanted to come clubbing with us. He seemed up for it, but a few of my sister's friends were a little worse for wear (Sheryl could barely stand and had to be given a fireman's lift by a passing gent) so we decided to give it a miss. Freddie walked us to the taxi rank and we said our goodbyes, with a promise that I would text him the next day.

On Saturday we arranged to meet near my home - he had very kindly let me choose the date venue, and so we went for a drink at a lovely old pub just outside the town. He had brought me roses, which was a very kind and romantic gesture. We chatted there for a while and eventually moved on to an Indian restaurant (even though neither of us was hungry) and talked about our jobs and interests. It seemed we had very little in common, and I think you really need things in common to be able to have a decent relationship with someone. But it was an enjoyable evening with some lovely company, and he's a real gentleman, and not a sex pest or a pervert.

I doubt that my sister's regular will become my favourite haunt, but I'm definitely up for another visit in the near future.

IS IT WORTH IT?

15/04/2014

One of my friends, Imogen has just started dating a new bloke called John. (It's Spring time. Love is rife!) In the run-up to their first date Imogen was panicked. From John's texts, and from speaking to him on the phone, she knew she was hooked, without ever having met him. Dangerous? Perhaps.
I was receiving message after message from her - she couldn't decide whether it was a good idea to go ahead with the date or not. What if she liked him too much? What if he didn't like her? What if she got her heart broken? What if all this emotion was for nothing? What if he was into butterflies? She was going to call it all off.

I had to talk her down from the metaphorical 'ledge' that she was threatening to jump from. Cancel the date? Was she mad? This was the first guy to make her feel this way in ages. Wasn't the chance of love worth the risk? I told her all this, but I'm not sure she bought it.

Imogen eventually decided to go ahead with her date, and she was very glad she did. They got on fantastically well, and had loads in common with each other.

He seemed just as nervous and just as keen on her. Thank goodness. But now she's worried that she's somehow going to screw it all up and lose him. (Sometimes you just can't win!) I've told her to relax, but she won't. She is still scared.

Whatever anyone says, you cannot protect yourself from heartbreak. There is no heart strong enough, no relationship secure enough, and no shield of steel or 'invisibility' cloak to defend you from love's effects. It's simply not possible to hide from it. But to deny yourself something that could be great, simply because you might get hurt sometime in the future? Best not to get into that line of thinking.
Everything ends eventually. Usually things that end, end in tears, there's nothing much you can do about that. That is the nature of life. On a relative scale we are here for a very short time. You should make the most of things while you can. You shouldn't go through life expecting things to end before they've even started. Love is worth everything we risk. That's why so many songs are written about it. It's what makes life worth living.

What about short term love? Relationships that you know can't last - are they worth the risk?

I think any love is worth the risk of a broken heart. I'm a firm believer in the saying 'Better to have loved and lost, than to never have loved at all.' I have lost many a love, and I don't regret having feelings for those people, even though with some of them the emotion couldn't be returned the way I wanted it to be. Sometimes you have to take what you can get and cherish the good memories that you're left with. Some people are not free to love you the way you want, but it doesn't mean there isn't feeling there. Love is a complicated beast.

Pain and heartbreak come with the territory and you have to accept that, if you want any chance of happiness. You've got to take the rough with the smooth, and accept that in life we don't always get what we deserve. You also shouldn't listen to anyone else's opinion when it comes to love. Let your heart decide what's right and what isn't. If you think you love someone, try to let them know, for tomorrow you may not get the chance.

FAILURE TO LAUNCH

28/04/2014

I know what you're thinking, but this post isn't about those men that have trouble in the bedroom. It's not about sex at all.   Well Ok, it's a little bit about sex, but it's not what you're thinking from the title.

Here's the scenario, gents... You've just arranged a first date with a woman that you're attracted to. Excellent, well done you for having the balls to ask her out (unless of course she beat you to it, moron!) You're very excited about the date. Your female friend is also very excited about your date. But what happens between setting it up and actually going on the date? You can seriously fuck up your chances with this woman with just one fell swoop. Want to hear how? Carry on reading, because as usual, chaps, I'm going to let you into a little secret...

You may be thinking that you can't wait to get this girl of yours into the sack, and maybe she's thinking the same...but wait - before you go telling her all the filthy details, STOP. Because you're about to make a fatal error of judgement. Women don't enjoy filthy chat with someone they hardly know. Actually most of the time they don't enjoy filthy chat with guys they do know either.

158

The secret - Most women are ruled by romance, not sex.

If you're texting your date before you meet, try not to go down the route of 'sexting' as it has recently come to be known, because it's unlikely to be a turn-on for your woman. I am generalising here, of course, some women might enjoy it, but the ones I speak to don't.

You can lose it very easily with some not-very-carefully chosen words. Let your heart (or your brain) do the thinking, and not your dick.

Here's a list of the sorts of things women want and don't want to hear from you, until you're intimately involved - after that, I'm sure you'll have a better idea of what it is they like.

Good (things that women like to hear)

- I miss you
- I can't wait to see you
- I would love to be seen with you / take you to dinner
- I want to hold your hand
- I want to hold you close
- You sound lovely
- If you get cold, you can borrow my jacket
- I don't know why you're still single
- You make me laugh
- You're so clever and interesting, I want to know you better

- My friends are jealous, because I get to go on a date with you

...or indeed anything remotely romantic that comes to mind

Bad (things that women don't want to hear)

- Your photo makes me horny
- Do you like to wear stockings?
- What are you wearing?
- I want to see you naked
- How big are your tits?
- I love your lips
- I want to get in your pants
- You're hot
- What would you do if you were locked in a room with me?

Very bad (don't ever do this, ever)

- Do you like to be spanked?
- I have a foot fetish
- I want to use your mouth as my play thing
- Do you swallow?
- Are you shaved?
- Will you sit on my face?
- My mate wants to shag you as well
- How do you feel about threesomes?

I could go on, but I'm sure you get the general idea.   When it comes to love, I understand that men are much more visual and physical than women, whereas women are turned on by what they hear, so don't forget that lads.

And if you really can't grasp what I'm getting at here, then you might be stuck 'playing lightsabers with Captain Solo' for a very long time to come.

SAYING GOODBYE

30/04/2014

As a firm believer in 'fate', as I've said before on this blog, I believe that people come into your life for a reason, and then when it's their time, they leave, and there's little you can do about it, but send them away with your love (or whatever emotion you prefer.) Sometimes goodbyes and break-ups end well, and sometimes you end up hating the former object of your affection with a passion and you just want to throw things at his or her head.

Shakespeare once wrote 'Parting is such sweet sorrow.' But what did Shakespeare know? Is parting a sweet sorrow, or is it a major heartache and gut-wrenching pain? I'm not sure 'Romeo and Juliet' would have been made any more palatable if Shakespeare had written it without his romantic bent, but I think had Juliet known that she wasn't going to see her beloved Romeo alive again, she would have said something more along the lines of 'Parting is such a major pain in the bollocks'.

Break-ups (and goodbyes) are hard. Not only for the person being broken up with, but for the person doing the breaking-up.

I know. I've been on both sides several times, and I know how difficult it can be to tell someone that you once loved (or, at least, thought you did) that the time has come to go your separate ways. It's the unpredictability of the situation that's really hard.

For one thing, you never know how they will react. Will they burst into tears? Laugh at you? Walk out the door without a second glance? Or threaten to throw themselves under a train? And what will you do when faced with any of those options? Will you give in to emotional blackmail, or stand your ground? Personally I prefer to stand my ground. There was only one instance where I did back down, but that wasn't because I'd changed my mind - my mind was set, I knew we weren't meant to be - but as I said sometimes you come into people's lives to make a difference, and the man in question needed a bit of a break. So I stayed with him until I felt he was sorted. Sometimes it's just your job to be there for someone who needs you.

What about when someone breaks up with you? Is that more or less difficult than doing the deed yourself? I once burst into tears in front of Owen, a guy I'd been dating for a few weeks, I don't remember the reason behind the tears, but I remember his reaction only too well.

He walked right out of my flat, without a backwards glance, and I never saw or heard from him again. Although that was pretty harsh and cowardly of him, at least it got me over him quickly. Long, drawn-out break-ups can be much harder, especially when you have to see your ex at work or as part of your social circle.

Are there good and bad ways to break up with someone? Yes. I feel it's always bad form to break up with someone you've been close to over email or text (or by Post-It note.) It's best to speak to them in person, or at least on the phone, to give them a chance to express how they feel about it.

What if their parting shot is ambiguous? What if you have no idea how they really feel about you because there's someone else in the picture? Your friends may tell you 'never go back' but sometimes that can be a difficult choice, especially if you do really have feelings for that person.
I say play it by ear, but don't settle for being someone's second best. You're better than that.

Saying 'goodbye' is never easy and you have to learn to accept that when someone has to leave, they have to leave. Acceptance is the first step to getting over them.

Deal with your feelings with dignity, let them go, and remember the good times. Try listening to some inspirational music - I always find solace in Queen's 'Another One Bites the Dust'. If that fails to make you feel any better, then I suggest a bottle of Tequila, a large tub of ice cream and a quick fling with someone completely inappropriate - it won't make you feel any better, but it might take the edge off and help you forget your plight for a few short moments.

Or you can try any of the following:

- Develop a crush on a fictional character eg. Benedict Cumberbatch as 'Sherlock'.
- Try your hand at archery / kickboxing / voodoo.
- Take up an instrument and learn how to play angry girl music.
- Become a lesbian (yes, you too Gents!) (Because we know you really want to!)
- Read your ex's horoscope and laugh when bad things are set to befall them.
- Remember (and talk about) their bedroom problems at every opportunity.
- Cook whatever you want - you're no longer stuck with a vegetarian / coeliac / mad German cannibal.
- Obsessively stalk them on Facebook (until they block you.)

- Ask for a hug. (Be careful who you choose though. Do not ask your therapist.)
- Look fucking fabulous everyday to remind your ex of what they're missing.
- Meet someone even more amazing and, when asked about your ex, say '[ex's first name] who?'

I saw this great quote on the internet recently....'Don't allow anyone to make more withdrawals on your life than deposits. Know when to close the account.' I think that sums it up pretty well.

LOST IN TRANSLATION

06/05/2014

After having been single for about the last 10 years (with the exception of that brief 4-week thing with Mike in Devon in 2007) I guess I am now in a relationship. Why am I guessing? Well, how do you know when 'just dating' turns into a 'relationship'? Because I have no idea. But as the man in question seems to be pretty committed and we've been dating for nearly 4 weeks now, I think it's safe to say.

So, who is this amazing man that has suddenly come out of nowhere, set my little heart a flutter, made me throw out the rule book and has managed against all odds to 'tame the shrew'? Well, I'll tell you if you just give me a chance. Jeez, you're just so impatient!

I mentioned in this blog, a few weeks ago, that I went out with my sister and her friends in Watford, and that she picked out a tall, dark, handsome man for me and beckoned him over to dance. Well, it turns out my sister has very good taste in men and I will probably never hear the end of this now, especially not from my nieces.

Freddie is 39 years old (a toyboy!) and he's originally from Kosovo. He's been in this country for 15 years and he works as a project manager in the construction industry (and apparently he's very nice to his workers.) He's also kind to me, he usually shows up with flowers or chocolates or a bottle of wine, and he really doesn't need to. He also has a very good sense of humour, which I've been trying to get a sense of, but so far we seem to laugh at the same kinds of things. He is not a vegetarian. All's good so far.

Where do we not see eye to eye? He loves politics and current affairs, and I hate all that lying, bullshit, nonsense. But this is not a deal-breaker.

We've seen a lot of each other over the last 4 weeks, and he calls me most days. He's not as keen on texting as I am, but that's because his English spelling isn't perfect - he spells the words as he pronounces them - but I usually tend to get the drift of what he's saying. Luckily his English is much better than my Kosovan (Albanian.) For example 'I coll you letter' is pretty obvious. Maybe it's something to do with him being European, but there appears to be no bullshit, no game playing, and when he can't be with me, he tells me he misses me. He calls me when he says he will. I like that.

I feel no need to analyse his every move, because it's all pretty straight forward. It's one of those WYSIWYG relationships, and I feel like I can finally breathe a sigh of relief.

On Saturday, apropos of nothing, while we were walking the dog, he told me something in confidence about himself, which I'm not going to divulge here - it was nothing worrying, but it simply proved to me that he considered me more than just a casual fling. I didn't have any major secrets to tell him, but I told him about my engagement and some past relationships. I haven't shown him the blog yet, but I did mention it to him, briefly, when we started dating. He also took me on a drive to a place where he hopes to lease premises and start a couple of businesses - he actually asked my opinion on what I thought of his ideas.

Without saying it aloud, I've tried to make him slowly aware that I see him as a 'serious proposition' (sounds rather business-like) and that I want him to feel secure, so I started learning Albanian. I can now say a few choice phrases, like 'Fasten your seatbelts, please.' Sometimes I text him in Albanian. Sometimes I even understand his response.

Albanian is like no other language I've ever spoken. It is completely alien. Like trying to learn Klingon. (NB. I can assure you, dear reader, that I have never tried to learn Klingon.) (Hab SoSlI Quch! - your mother has a smooth forehead!) (I Googled that, I promise.)

I've also been teaching him some very British colloquialisms that he wasn't aware of. For example 'The Dog's Bollocks' (testiseve qeni) - he had been under the impression that it was a bad thing and meant the opposite of what it actually means. When he swears in English it's very funny - 'fockin wenkas'.

I'm sure that quite a bit of what we say to each other gets lost in translation, especially on the phone, but his texts are usually fairly easy to understand. Some of them have me in stitches. I've come to learn that:

I look foreword to met you Aegean = I'm looking forward to meeting you again

I coming end duet for you = I'll come and do it for you

Shoo mi haw = show me how

Mi friend don now nothing his dungy - (this one took a while to get to the bottom of) = my friend doesn't know nothing, he's a donkey!

Still sloping = still sleeping

Vary nays = very nice

In the shaver = in the shower

My dog is fascinated by him. He's not had a lot of experience of me dating anyone as he's only 7. When Freddie and I are sitting on the sofa together, my dog jumps up and tries to squeeze his fat little bottom between the two of us - it doesn't matter how close we're sitting, he will always try to wiggle his way in between. This has caused much hilarity - not so much for the dog, as he tends to get scooped up and put back on the floor - where he will then make several attempts to get back on the sofa.

When he does get back up, he is placed to either side of us, but always jumps back over and tries to squeeze back in the middle again. And so it goes on.

It makes a nice change not to be writing about bad dates. Long may it continue.

DATING AND TECHNOLOGY

15/05/2014

It has long been my belief that technology and dating do not good bedfellows make. And although I'm a bit of a gadget-girl myself, I do not necessarily believe that technology is our friend. The younger generation will of course wonder how we managed in the 'olden days' (or earlier than 1992) before iPads, instant messaging, and Twitter.

What the hell did we do before smart phones and Facebook? How did we arrange to meet people while on the move? How did we see what our beloved was up to when he or she wasn't with us? How did we stalk our crushes? Well, the fact was, we did it all the old fashioned way. We made arrangements on the landline phone, and we kept those arrangements unless there was an emergency. We didn't cancel on friends at the last minute by text, simply because we could. If we were worried about a loved one cheating on us, we checked their pockets, or hired a detective, or threatened them with the loss of a vital organ. We stalked our crushes in person, by standing outside their house and staring through their living room window. I am joking, of course. (The bedroom window is always better!)

But let's look at the more serious side of our reliance on social networking sites like Facebook, and Twitter. We are now barraged by a wealth of information. Too much information... Information that can so easily be used against us.

In the days before Facebook, we never needed to worry about the status of our loved ones...Who they were poking, or who was poking them. Ignorance was bliss. We had no need for the constant status updates and navel-gazing that 'social networking' has made commonplace. The reliance on the internet has made it possible for people to lie about who they are, to easily arrange casual hook-ups, marital affairs etc etc. Is it any wonder that in the UK, almost one in two marriages now ends in divorce?

I put 'social networking' in inverted commas because I believe it keeps us from being social. Having 200 online 'friends' doesn't make you any less lonely when you really need a special someone to talk to. Now put down that iPhone and have an actual conversation.

As you already know from my writings, I've had plenty of experience of online dating sites. I've met people who found it necessary to lie about themselves in some way - sometimes just small ways like about how tall they were (or whether they were interested in butterflies) which is no big deal – but for others, the internet seems to be a portal for them to act out their fantasy lives, to lie about who they really are, to con people into having feelings for them. For what reason they feel the need to do this, who can say? Maybe it's an ego boost for them. Maybe it brightens up their miserable lives in some strange way. But I say again, Technology has not made dating any less painful. You may think it's now easier to hook up with anyone you fancy, but just how easy is it to trust that person?

Technology is not your friend.

FINGERS CROSSED, I JUST BOUGHT LINGERIE

19/05/2014

Previously (in my life)... I got a new boyfriend, and regular readers will know how amazed I am about that particular fact. I've been so out of the loop in relationship matters that I had forgotten how much time, effort and money it takes trying to look salon-perfect (not a chance!) every bloody day (on the off-chance that he's coming over) and making sure that my partner's tastes are catered for. I don't mean to be crude, but this relationship is already costing me a fortune in make-up, Peroni and protection.

Also, apropos of my new relationship, I've just been out and bought some new lingerie. I mentioned what happens with my boyfriends when I buy lingerie - usually they run away. So, fingers crossed on this one.

The other worrying thing is that my birthday is coming up. No, I'm not particularly concerned about being another year older, especially as most people meeting me wrongly assume that I'm somewhere in the region of 32.

What does worry me is this... my family are having a birthday dinner for me at the weekend, and they have told me that my new boyfriend is invited too.

This strikes the fear of God into me. Not because I want to keep Freddie from meeting my folks, but because he would have to endure The Spanish Inquisition and the questions about what he does or doesn't eat. (Luckily he's not vegetarian. This is a first for me.)
He has already met my sister, and as she's the one who picked him out, but he would also have to endure my nieces asking him 'Are you going to marry Shazzy?' (That's 'Auntie Shazzy' to you!) The possibilities for embarrassment are endless. And what with English not being his first language, I doubt he would thank me.

So I gave Freddie a choice. On the phone, I originally just told him to keep the date free, and then when I saw him at the weekend, I explained, and asked him if he was ready to come along and endure the humiliation, (though not in those words) or if he'd rather wait and endure it at a later date. He opted for the later date option, which I can totally appreciate.

Being back in a relationship has made me realise just how uptight they make me feel - I now remember why I have avoided them for so long. I become completely irrational and panicky. Now I am gripped with the fear of having 'something to lose', as fate has never been kind to me where relationships have been concerned. So much simpler when I was single and didn't have anything to lose. Not to say that it's not wonderful, having somebody around, because it is, I just wish I was better at not caring. But I do care.

So let's hope that the lingerie has the desired effect, and not the 'Weeeee! Off they run' effect.

A really bad poem to end...

In a bid to impress a man
I try to do whatever I can
To coax him into matrimony
As long as he doesn't keep mascarpone
And if you want a man to stay
You can't beat sexy lingerie
Half-cup, full-cup, balconette
Bras and panties and corset
Stockings and suspender belts
Ensures their hearts will surely melt.

FRIENDS, LOVERS, OR NOTHING?

20/05/2014

A couple of weeks ago, my friend Imogen asked me for advice about a guy that she recently met on a date. He'd looked 'good on paper', they had a lot in common, had similar senses of humour, and she thought he was a 'really nice guy'. The problem (apart from the state of his teeth and the massive whitehead on his chin, which she couldn't stop starting at) was that she didn't fancy him in the slightest. How could this be?

He had felt chemistry, or so he claimed, in the numerous texts that he sent her post-date. So why couldn't she feel the same? Was it just the whitehead? Or was there really no chemistry between them at all? The thing with chemistry is, you can't force it. It's either there or it isn't. Though chemistry can grow out of feeling nothing, but you have to give the relationship time. You have to be friends first.

How do you know if a friendship is likely to develop into something more? Well, for me, it's about commonality in the relationship, finding things that you both like (butterflies?) sharing a sense of humour (whiteheads are funny).

It's also about admiration and respect (I admire the fact that you seem to have self-confidence despite the ugly whitehead on your face.) Looks take on less importance when you really get to know someone. Take Shrek and Fiona as an example. Ok, I know they're just animated characters, but it is possible to fall in love with someone that you once may have found less than attractive, if their personality has a lovable side to it.

Sometimes it just takes spending a bit of time together to make sparks fly.
How long does it take to become more than friends? (How long is that whitehead going to be around?) That's like asking 'how long is a piece of string?' Who can say? It's totally dependant on how much time you spend with that person, how much of yourself you show and whether or not you're really compatible. Your crush may immediately put you in the 'friend zone' and from there, it can be near impossible to escape.

So from my own experience, have I had friends that I wanted to turn into lovers? Of course I have, on many occasions. Some of which happened, and some of which didn't. One particular long-time friend, after we eventually got it together, decided after 3 days that he couldn't hack it.

Something about him feeling 'unable to keep me in the manner to which I had become accustomed' or some such bollocks. I don't need a man to 'keep' me, just love me. Unfortunately our friendship suffered as a result and hasn't been the same since.

And what about the reverse? Did any of my male friends want to make more of a relationship with me, when I wanted to keep it platonic? Yes they did, dear reader. I've been in a couple of situations with good male friends where they wanted to take it further, but I wasn't so sure. I had already placed them firmly in the friend zone and felt no sexual chemistry with either of them. One of them, who was newly single, had invited me back to his place after a day out, and as we sat together, talking on his sofa, I remember getting some very odd vibes from him. My exit time, from his house to my car, could have rivalled Mo Farah, such was my desire to keep him just as a friend, and luckily he and I are still close. But would we have still been friends if I'd slept with him? I can't say. Of course eventually they all get married, and it's far better to have 'plausible deniability' when you have the 'have you slept with any of your friends of the opposite sex' conversation, especially if you want your spouse to still allow you to be friends with that person.

———

180

What if neither a friendship nor a relationship develop? Then you have to let them go on their way and understand that it wasn't to be. Stay classy and don't give in to hurt feelings by giving them a piece of your mind, or a taste of your temper. Don't post dog shit through their letterbox or anything like that. You may live to regret it.

WEE...OFF THEY RUN!

03/09/2014

It's been a while since I wrote a blog post, and that's because I was in a happy relationship...at least I thought I was. But, as always, the minute I bought lingerie, it was a case of 'weeeee, off they run!' As soon as I thought we were OK, it all started to fall apart.

After 2 months of dating Freddie (the Kosovan) I was comfortable enough to assume that our relationship was serious. He was confiding in me, telling me about his life and work, the daughter that he'd hardly seen in Kosovo, his ambitions for starting his own business, and asking me how I felt about marriage and children. I thought I was pretty safe.

On our last date, he took me out for dinner (he'd managed to get a screw in his tyre, so I insisted on driving.) At the restaurant he asked me how I felt about marriage and children. I said I wanted to get married one day and I asked him how he felt. He said it wasn't the piece of paper that was important, but the relationship, which I thought was quite a strange thing to say.

He stayed over that night, and he'd told me he had to go and pick up his sister at the airport early the next morning. In the morning he woke up later than planned and said 'Oh shit!'

He dashed out of the house and I didn't realise that that would be the last time I would see him. A few days later, I got a text from him saying that his visa had expired and he was back in Kosovo trying to sort it. He said it would take about 2 weeks. At first I was pissed off that he hadn't told me, but he said it had been an emergency, and so I was willing to overlook the delayed communication. The 2 weeks went by and he told me that his visa application had been denied and he was going to have to appeal. He said he was very angry, but he was seeing a solicitor to see what could be done. He said that the solicitor was hopeful that it would all be sorted and it was just a case of waiting. I asked if there was anything I could do to help, and what if the appeal failed, and he said that the only other chance would be for him to marry a British person.

Knowing that he was the kind of guy that I would have happily married (being 43 and still unmarried) I offered, but he didn't jump at the chance. I felt this was a good sign, that he wasn't just dating me for a visa. We stayed in contact over the next few weeks as he waited for any news on his visa appeal. I knew it could take months before the appeal was heard, but I was prepared to wait for him as long as he wanted me to. We spoke on the phone a couple of times, and texted often. Our last conversation in mid-July, he told me he was having trouble with his phone and I said that if he was still stuck in Kosovo when the summer holidays started, that I would come out and visit him.

After that I texted still, but wasn't getting any replies back. I figured he'd probably decided not to pursue our relationship any longer, so I sent him a long text telling him that I cared about him very much but I needed to know how he felt and if he still wanted to continue our relationship. He phoned me straight away and said he felt the same way about me and he was hoping to get the visa as soon as he could so he could get back home and see me. He was also considering trying to get a visa for France.

Another month went past and I was getting fed up of waiting for news. It had all gone quiet again and my texts were going unanswered. I tried a last ditch attempt to get in contact - I told him that if he was still having communication issues to get one of his family in the UK to contact me and let me know what was happening.

The next day, while I was driving down to Dorset to meet my friend for a camping trip, I got a phone call from someone claiming to be Freddie's brother, Arnie. He told me that Freddie had been very angry at the delay in getting his visa, and got himself into some trouble with the British Embassy in Albania. Apparently he'd got into a fight with a security guard and had landed himself in prison - Arnie said he'd been sentenced to 2 years! But said that his solicitor was working to appeal and get him out. I was in shock.

I didn't sleep at all that night and my best friend had to deal with me bursting into tears every few minutes as we debated whether it was likely to be true, and what to do about it if it was.

I texted Arnie, to find out a little more, and I quizzed him to get as much information as I could. He said he didn't know which prison Freddie was in, or the name of his solicitor, but he said that his little brother, Tommy, in Kosovo was keeping hold of Freddie's phone and would let him know if there was any news. This was all very strange. I'd managed to get the correct spelling on Freddie's surname from his brother, it was one letter out from what Freddie had already told me was his surname. So I did myself a little bit of internet research...

I hadn't visited Freddie at his house - he'd said he lived with a couple of lodgers and that he'd have to tidy before I came round - that was his excuse, and I was quite happy for him to come round to my place.   But knowing his full name, I was able to do a proper search for him. I knew approximately where he lived in Wembley, and I found a listing for him there, along with a house mate – Edwina Caras. I looked up Edwina on Facebook and sent her a message asking if she was the same woman that lived with Freddie. I said I was a friend of his and asked if she could call me. (She never did) At the same time, I also looked up his brothers on Facebook - I found all of them (3 of them) and added the youngest, Tommy, as a friend. He messaged me instantly, and I began asking him about Freddie. He didn't seem to know who I was, and said that Freddie was in London and not in Albania as I had been told. He didn't know I was Freddie's girlfriend. Alarm bells immediately rang.

I then looked through Edwina's Facebook photos and found photos of her with Freddie. No mention of their relationship, I assumed that this was the sister that he said he owned the house with.

More digging and I found a marriage record for the two of them! He was married, with a 5-year-old daughter!

___

My friend Imogen knew someone who could help with a little more digging on the immigration side, and her friend was able to pull up records to show that Freddie had never left the country and had been in the UK the whole time while I was worried sick about him.

I had insomnia from being so anxious, and lost nearly a stone in weight because I was unable to eat properly.

To say I felt totally betrayed would be an understatement. I couldn't believe that I'd been duped by someone I totally trusted, and it had been 10 years since I'd trusted anyone enough to have a relationship with them.

I didn't know what to do about it - of course, part of me wanted revenge at any cost - I wanted to go over to his house and knee him in the nuts, or give him a matching set of tyres with screws in them - but I had no desire to sink to his level, or to do anything to hurt his family. I decided instead to text him the following message...

'Hi Freddie, I don't know exactly why you've found it necessary to lie to me and treat me the way you have, but no one deserves to have this done to them. I know you've lied about everything.

I now know that you're married with a child and that you never left the UK in June. I also know where you live (13 ***** Road) I would suggest that you give me a call in the next couple of days and give me a full explanation of why you've done this.'

I don't expect to hear anything from him, but if it's put the wind up him at all, then I feel my work here is done. Of course I should have seen the signs, but you live and learn and try not to make the same mistakes.

Now I'm single again and it's time to move on.

TELL TALE SIGNS

12/09/2014

So, previously, my beloved and trusted boyfriend, Freddie, turned out to be a lying, cheating, adulterous bastard. He kept his pretence up for 5 months (3 of which he claimed to be abroad, when in fact he was still in London.) I still have no idea exactly why he led me on for so long, but I do have a few theories...

1. It was just an affair, which either ended when his wife found out or when he decided I was getting too close that I might find out. (In which case why lie to me for the following 3 months?)

2. It was all about a residency visa... The woman to whom he is married, is a Greek national (don't ask me how I know this) and therefore has residency status under EEC laws, but as a Kosovan married to a Greek, I'm assuming he does not get automatic residency. He also has a child who was born in this country and therefore has a UK passport. Was his intent to ditch the wife for a couple of years, marry a British citizen, gain his own citizenship and then get divorced and go back to the original wife? In this case his wife would have to be in on the plan. Why did he break it off when he did? Because his visa got renewed for another 2 years.

3. Was the intent some sort of con game which never came to fruition because I found him out?

It's all so complicated. 5 months of deception, stories and lies. The expired visa, the refusal of a renewal, the promise of an appeal, trouble at the embassy, a prison sentence - In Albania!!
...A web of deceit so complex to unravel, it would make Benedict Cumberbatch's Sherlock Holmes break out in a sweat.
My friend Amanda made a highly amusing comment while we were sat around discussing the situation. She said something along the lines of 'You've got to give it to these Eastern Europeans, they're hard workers!' - and even though I was at my lowest ebb, I nearly laughed myself under the table. Even my 13 year-old niece got in on the act, by making a Wanted poster. 'Dead or Alive. Reward £2.99.'
Everyone's a comedian.

But which of my three theories is the correct one? Maybe none. I guess I will probably never find out, which is a shame, because the mystery is keeping me awake at night. Going over and over every little detail. I have a feeling it's the second option, which would mean his wife is equally to blame. Who would do that to someone? How would they feel if someone treated their daughter that way?

Should I have seen any tell-tale signs that he was already married, or that he was spinning me a tall tale?

I won't say I didn't have any niggles during the so-called 'relationship' - I often berated him for never pre-warning me that we were going out to dinner, for which he always paid with cash. He always showed up with flowers or chocolates, or both. His phone was never in existence in my presence. We never spent a full 24-hours together, though he did often stay overnight. This to me suggests that either his wife was away for the 2 months we dated, that he lied to her about doing night-shift work, or that she was well aware of the whole situation. I can't decide which is worse.

So what are the tell-tale signs that the man you're dating is married?

1. Does he make excuses why you can't come over to his place? Does he refuse to give you his address? Does he lie about his address? (see below for details of 192.com)

2. Does he only phone you at certain times? Does he only call you from work? Does he answer the phone when you call? Is there always a delay for him to text or call you back?

3. Does he wear a ring? Is there an indentation on his ring finger? Is there a ring-shaped indentation in his wallet or his pocket?

4. When he's out with you, does he pay by cash? Are his credit cards only in his name, or is his wife's name on them also? Does he leave the receipts at the restaurant?

5. Watch for strange behaviour on dates...does he disappear when his phone rings? Does he have more than one phone?

6. Does he give strange reasons for not wanting to go to certain places?

7. Does he give strange or implausible reasons why he can't make a date? Car crash? Hospitalisation? His dog is sick? His grandma in Cornwall has an in-growing toenail?

8. Does he shower you with gifts - flowers, chocolates, adjustable wrenches? Trying to assuage his guilt perhaps?

If you're in any doubt, do some investigative work of your own. For a small charge 192.com publishes details of everyone on the electoral register, their address, their approximate age, and the names and ages of the adults they live with.

You can also get more in depth information from their site by paying slightly more.   Once you have names of other people living at the same address, try an internet or Facebook search for them. Ancestry.co.uk will have marriage records that can be searched, or may appear on Google once you search for the names involved. You can uncover all sorts online. Failing that, if you're really serious, you can hire a Private Detective. You could, of course, ask him straight out if he is married. If he is lying you can look out for the following clues - he hesitates, breaks eye contact briefly, touches his earlobe or nose, or clears his throat before answering.

For those of you who are married, here are the tell-tale signs of whether your spouse is cheating on you:

1. They are suddenly plying you with thoughtful gifts.

2. Their work patterns change and they start working a lot more overtime, weekends etc.

3. They are less tactile or passionate than usual.

4. They are hiding their mobile phone from you.

5. They are receiving texts or calls at odd times.

6. They suddenly start wearing nicer clothes / underwear / perfume or taking more care of their appearance.

7. They claim to have a new friend or group of friends, and you're not invited.

8. They've started a new hobby or joined a new club, but can produce no evidence of this.

Most importantly trust your instincts. If you think something is wrong, then something is probably wrong. I remember complaining about Freddie, to my friend Imogen, on more than one occasion, 'I don't know why he likes me.' I felt he had no appreciation of the person I was, especially when I compared his view of me to someone that I knew really liked me for me. I should have trusted that.

Statistically, 1 in 3 men listed on online dating sites is married. That's a big statistic, and a scary thought. It doesn't make life any easier for those of us who are single, honest, good-natured and always willing to see the best in people, no matter how much we've been hurt in the past.

There were things about Freddie that I really loved. If he had turned out not to be a lying, cheating, wanker, he would have actually made a very nice husband. But I don't know if most of what he told me was the truth or all lies. I always assumed he was telling the truth.

CHOCOLATE FINGERS

18/09/2014

I just got to thinking recently how first dates and job interviews have a lot in common. For a start there are the nerves, the butterflies in the stomach... oh no, not butterflies again, Sharon! Do you have a thing about butterflies? No, dear reader, I do not, they have just become a bit of a running joke. Like mascarpone cheese, and Marwell zoo.

We get nervous about first dates for the same reason that we get nervous about interviews... We only get one chance to impress, and will be judged on first sight. What will the person sitting opposite think of me? Will they like me? What will they ask me? Will there be any trick questions? It's always good to prepare for the unexpected. Think fast...

'If you were a biscuit, what kind of biscuit would you be?'
'I'd be a chocolate finger!'
'Why?' (Shit! I didn't think that one through before answering!)
'Erm, because I'm straight and like having chocolate licked off me.' Godammit.
Or 'I'm a Wagon Wheel' - A biscuit with many layers, all of them good.

Just make sure you engage your brain before answering questions like those. Of course if this were a date, or you were interviewing for the role of Porn Star, then the chocolate finger line might just pay off!

When it comes to relating yourself to certain biscuits, be careful what you choose...
Jaffa Cake – I'm schizophrenic, and I refuse to be pigeon-holed. I don't know who I am or what I want. I like to seem mysterious, but my mystery is all revealed in one bite. I live my life on Facebook.

Digestive – I'm straight-talking, practical, down-to-earth, and always reliable. At home I wear slippers.

Hobnob – I seem strong, but I crumble easily under pressure. Sometimes I like to wear my wife's underwear, but only when she's not around.

Chocolate finger – I'm a dirty pervert!

Custard Cream – I'm sensible and modest. My favourite singer is Michael Bublé. In bed, I like the missionary position.

Pink Wafer – I've got great taste in home furnishings, I like line dancing as a hobby, and I've got a tub of mascarpone cheese in the fridge for just in case.

Toffeepop – Let's not even go there!

In certain interview situations, you might get asked which animal you are: a chameleon, a wolf or an owl.
'I'm a chameleon.'
'Why?'
'Because if you dress me in tartan, I explode.'
Wrong answer.
The chameleon is able to adapt to changing situations. The wolf is a go-getter, hungry and predatory. The owl has a head that can swivel 360 degrees. Or maybe it's just very wise, I forget now. Anyway you probably won't want to use the 'swivel 360 degrees' line unless you're either auditioning for a role in a remake of 'The Exorcist', or you want to work in Air-Traffic Control.
The kind of questions that you're likely to get in either situation share a lot in common. They are designed to find out if you are the person best suited to the job, or best suited to the needs of your date.   So how do the classic interview questions relate to dating? I'll show you...

What the interviewer wants to know, followed by the dating equivalent subtext:

Why do you want this job?   (Why do you want a relationship with me?)

What do you have to offer?   (Are you great in the kitchen and bedroom?)

Where do you see yourself in 5 years' time?   (Are you expecting marriage, or can I get away with some casual sex?)

Why did you leave your last job?   (Why did your last boyfriend leave you?)

Tell me about yourself   (Tell me about yourself, without referencing your ex. Include any sexual fantasies)

Are you flexible?   (Are you an experimental lover?)

How do you cope with pressure?   (Do you throw things when you get PMT?)

What is your dream job?   (Do you like cooking, cleaning and ironing?)

What kind of person do you find difficult to work with?   (Are you open to my foot fetish?)

Are you willing to travel with work? (Have you ever been to Marwell Zoo?)
The interviewer wants to know that you have skills, experience and enthusiasm for the job. Your date will want to know that you will fit in with their interests, cater to their needs and satisfy them sexually.

But Sharon, I hear you ask, how will I know how to answer the really difficult questions? If in doubt, just be really vague, don't commit yourself, especially if you really like them and are worried about being judged harshly. You don't want your date knowing everything about you the first time you meet. You need to leave room for a little mystery. For example, I seldom tell men with whom I am on a first date, that I write a comedy dating blog. You can see how that might turn them off! (Of course if I've suddenly decided that I don't want to meet them, I give them the URL and that usually does the trick!)

In the dating situation, (if you are a woman) you basically need to ascertain what kind of girl your date is after, and pretend to be that person until you are safely wed. Then, and only then, can you reveal your true colours and admit to having no interest in anything they like. And admit to writing a comedy dating blog.

Of course, I jest. You should never lead someone on in any way, just because you fancy them. You should always aim to date / marry someone that you do actually have something in common with, even if it's just a love of chocolate fingers. They should also be appreciative of your comedy dating blog.

When I say 'appreciative' I mean that they should appreciate that they never appeared in one.

"TAKE ME TO BED, OR LOSE ME FOREVER"

24/09/2014

You know that your evening out with a former Navy pilot (hence the 'Top Gun' reference) is about to take a nose-dive, when your date starts to try and explain the concepts of matter and energy to you, and adamantly refuses to believe that a particular genre of television actually exists.
Let me back track a little...

So, last night I had a date with Lorrenzo, who is originally from Spain and works in the Forces. We'd met on an online dating site and had been text chatting for a couple of weeks while he was out on business in the Middle East. He got back a couple of days ago and we arranged to meet at an Indian restaurant I used to know well, somewhere in Middlesex, where I was brought up.   I arrive and get a text from him saying he's in the pub opposite, with drink in hand, so I go to find him. He half-heartedly offers to buy me one, but as I am up anyway I say it's Ok, and I go buy my own. The first half hour of the date is fairly painful. We seem to have very little in common to talk about. He isn't that chatty and makes himself thoroughly disagreeable.

I'm thinking about making my excuses, when he suggests we move on to the restaurant. Great, I'm hungry.

The first hour in the restaurant, is excruciating. He is clearly of the opinion that he knows best about every subject under the sun, which of course he doesn't. He talks complete bollocks, as a little secret smile (smirk) plays across my lips, telling the waiters that, yes, I know I am in the company of a knobhead. He orders first, not asking me what I want (not a sign of chivalry) He wants water, no starters and no poppadums. (What kind of insanity is this???) So I order a poppadum just to spite him.
When my single poppadum arrives I kindly (and against all feelings to the contrary) offer him half, but he declines, saying it's Ok, I should eat while he talks. (Kill me now!)

He starts talking about how we, as a planet, would go about sending spaceships to distant stars, and that we'd either have to put someone into deep hibernation for hundreds of years, or (and this is a direct quote) 'download their brains into a robot.' He says that would be the only way of exploring interstellar space. So I mention wormhole travel and bending space time, but in his opinion, that isn't possible! (But downloading a human brain into a robot he has no problem with!!) Inside, I sigh and beg the universe for some kind of mercy.

I had mentioned to him previously about my interest in the paranormal and how I had lived in a haunted house for 5 years, where objects would move around by themselves and lights would switch on with no one there etc. He had told me that when we met he would tell me something about that. So I wait with bated breath...

He points to his knife on the table:
'This is a knife...' (Glad we got that one sorted out, because I was confused up until that point.)
'It's made of matter.' (Physics 101?)
'This is my finger...and it's also made of matter.' (I thought if I told him 'There is no knife' that his brain might explode, so I didn't.)
'When I push the knife with my finger, it moves...' (Jesus Christ is this going somewhere?) I nod, patiently.
'But it's the electrons in my fingers, which have a negative charge, repelling the electrons in the knife, which also have a negative charge.' (eh?)
'But something else is also required, and that's energy.' (Ok)
'And that's how I can move the knife. But if there is no matter and no energy, then you cannot move the knife. So an entity that is not made of matter cannot move anything.' (or something along those lines.) (And here's where I step in...)

'But...' I say, '...matter and energy can convert, one to the other...' (and here's where I bring out the big guns) '...as in Einstein's equation for the conservation of energy, $E=mc^2$, which states not only that matter can be converted to energy but also that the reverse is possible - energy can be converted into matter...' That stops him in his tracks as he slowly begins to realise that this 'little woman' in front of him clearly understands more about quantum mechanics and than he does. He quickly changes the subject.

Eventually he relaxes enough to let me get a few words in, so I start telling him about some of my bad dates. I tell him about Freddie. I tell him about '2-hour man' and how when my allotted time was up, he looked at his watch and said, 'Well, you've had your 2 hours.' And I tell him about the tub of mascarpone that Cheesecake man kept in his fridge for emergencies. I laugh about it all, but he doesn't seem to have much of a sense of humour. I tell him that I've been trying to write a comedy drama series, and he says it can either be drama or comedy, but not both. (At this point I smile because I am envisioning strangling him with his own intestines). And what the hell does he know about television anyway?

Then he starts trying to touch my hands across the table, which comes as a bit of a shock to me, because I felt certain, by this point, that we weren't getting along. (But then my character judgements have been rather off this year.)

Thank Christ the date finally ends, and as he's walked because his car has a flat battery, I offer to drive him back to his flat, which he accepts. Thankfully he doesn't try to kiss me goodbye, but tells me he'll text me tomorrow.
I'm not sure that he's sensible enough to not want to meet up again, but if he does ask, I might just go, if only for the entertainment value, and the fact that I could do with a really good argument right now.

"...YOU DON'T WANT TO DIE SINGLE, DO YOU?"

28/09/2014

I said in my last post, that if Lorrenzo foolishly decided that he wanted to go on another date with me, that I would probably go, if only for the entertainment value. Well, guess what? A couple of days after our date, he texted me (he was clearly expecting to hear from me first!) and asked me if I'd go out to dinner with him again. So I said Ok. Here's what happened:

We arrange to go to a Thai restaurant near my home, as he's never had Thai food before and it's my favourite. He had wanted to pick me up from my house, hoping no doubt that he would get an invitation to come in for 'coffee' after dinner, but as I had no plans to ever see him again after this date, I thought I'd tell him to meet me near the restaurant.
We get seated at the restaurant and there are some Thai prawn crackers on the table. Great, I love Thai crackers. I begin eating them, while I quiz him about what level of spicy heat he can manage. He only likes mild. (Wimp.) I offer the Thai crackers, but he doesn't want any.
So I continue eating them and trying to make conversation, as at this point he is just staring at me, and saying nothing.

So there I am, munching crackers and talking about food, and suddenly he grabs my right hand and pulls it down on to the table and says 'You're constantly moving and talking. Is that because you're nervous or really hungry?' I say 'A bit of both.'

So he snatches the basket of prawn crackers away out of my reach and tells me to keep still. (At this point I'm looking down at my knife and wondering how long I can hold off before stabbing him in the eye.) So I sit still, arms crossed in front of me and mime zipping up my mouth. Then he says 'You can still talk.' I say 'No, I'm going to sit here and just be still and quiet.' So I sit and just stare at him for a minute. Two can play at that game.

Before our starters arrive, he grabs both my hands, puts them on the table in front of him and alarmingly starts caressing them. He tells me he can tell I take good care of my hands because they're so soft. I tell him that I don't take care of my hands in any way, that I'm always breaking my nails and getting cuts and bruises because of the nature of my job. He says he thought I worked in front of a computer (shows how much attention he pays) so I then have to explain again about what I actually do. He then turns my hands over in his, examining me for scars! He even starts rolling up my sleeves!

He says he can't find any, so I end up showing him some little scars on my hands. He says he'll find more 'later', and I'm thinking 'No you f*cking won't, you presumptious little tw*t!'
I manage to regain possession of my hands and ask him about what scares him. He says 'I have all my fears under control apart from one.' I ask what. He says 'cockroaches.' I ask him what his other fears are, and he says 'being underwater.'

I ask him about what he likes about his job and he answers 'the money'. It's the kind of soulless response that I was expecting from him. This is a man who appears to have no real interests and takes no enjoyment from anything. He is just an eating, talking, breathing machine.
Then he says something quite unexpected. He says 'I've been thinking about this a lot recently...' so I'm thinking he has something deep and meaningful to say... 'In a zombie apocalypse, what would you do? Would you stay at home?' (This is exactly the sort of question my friend Imogen would love) and I start to answer, telling him that I'd be out there

killing zombies, when he interrupts, saying 'Nothing, because we'd all be dead in 10 minutes.' (He really has no intention of hearing what anybody else has to say.) Then he goes on to explain about the nuclear power plants shutting down and radioactive water getting into the water supply and everybody dying. At this point I change the subject and ask him how the stir fried chicken is.

At the (long awaited) end of the meal we get the bill and he doesn't even offer to pay for me, which is fine because as I wasn't intending to see him again, I would have declined anyway. But it would have been nice if he'd offered, seeing as he asked me out to dinner. I take one of the chocolate mints and eat it, and as he doesn't want his, he offers it to me and says 'For later'. I take it and start to unwrap it. And he stops me, saying 'No. For later.' (No idea what he had planned for later, and how it would involve a chocolate mint) So just in spite of him, I defiantly give him my shark eyes stare and fixed smile, whilst continuing to slowly unwrap the chocolate. I sweetly place it in my mouth and chew. Silently telling him that I do not take orders.

He says he fancies a walk, so I take him on a walk through my home town, pointing out the local attractions 'Here's another Indian restaurant...here's Subway...here's the train station.' etc and all the time he has his hand around the back of my neck (I kid you not!) And I'm wondering how I'm going to get rid of him. At the end of the shops, I do an about turn and start heading back for the car park. It seems like an eternity but eventually we arrive at the car, and he's clearly waiting for an invitation back to mine, but he gets none. I say thanks for the evening and I wish him goodnight.

I would rather die single in a zombie apocalypse than to spend another moment in this man's company!

THE THINGS I HAVE LEARNED

Dating is a bit of a game. The term 'game' is defined as 'an activity that one engages in for amusement.' OK, so most of the time dating isn't that amusing, especially when you're trying your best to find your perfect partner and coming up against a brick wall each and every time. But there are times, as demonstrated in this book, when dating is amusing, especially if you don't treat it too seriously.

When you've been involved with playing a game of sport over a long period of time, you learn a lot of things. There are the rules, for a start, what you can and can't do, no hand balls, the off-side rule etc. There's also the familiarity – you learn the way that other players play, the way that some players break the rules, what you can do when the referee isn't watching. Well, the same is true with dating, once you've spent a few years at it, you come to know where your strengths lie and how the match is won.

So what are the top 10 things I have learned from my twenty-odd years playing the dating game?

1. Apparently there are no rules to dating. Though there should be. There's no

referee on the sidelines making sure that everything is done by the book, punishing those that break the moral codes and take advantage of the naive romantics. Wouldn't it be great if there were a superhero called 'The Adulterator' – a sort of Terminator for adulterers, who could swoop in on big motorcycle, wearing black leathers and brandishing an AK-47, ready to deal out punishments on the cheaters?

2. Never trust that is man is either single or straight just because he is on a dating site looking for a woman. Ideally, do not sleep with him until you have seen his place. If he won't allow you to see his place, there's a strong chance he's married. If you go to his place and find he has excellent taste in home furnishings, question him further regarding his intentions. If you find mascarpone in his fridge then get the hell out of there as fast as possible, or make the most of his good style and invite him on a clothes shopping trip with you and your gal pals.

3. If a man starts asking you about your fantasies or cup size or getting into any kind of sex chat with you before you've even met, log off / walk away / shut down. They are not after a serious

relationship. They are petting the porpoise at your expense.

4. The way to a man's heart is not via his stomach. We've all been told this at some point, but it wasn't just for that reason that I learned to cook like a demon - I've always been a big fan of food anyway - but I hoped that it might help win the love of a good man if I could cook him a nice meal. But at age 43 I have had to concede, that the way to a man's heart has absolutely nothing to do with his stomach. However, if you treat a man well and he still doesn't want to be with you, move on, it just isn't to be.

5. There are not plenty more fish in the sea, unless you actually want to date a monkfish. As they say a good man is hard to come by (and a hard man is good to come by!) but finding a good, honest man in the singles dating pool is like trying to find a pair of sheer tights that don't ladder on the first wear. Cast your net wide.

6. If there's a guy you're interested in, there are a number of 'ploys' you can try to get him to make a move. There's the 'getting a bit tipsy' ploy – pretend to be more tipsy than you are in his company, and

get him to walk you home, or aid you in some other way. The 'I'm cold' ploy – forget to bring your jacket, shiver a bit, and if he's interested, he'll put an arm around you or offer you his jacket. The 'massage' ploy – tell him you've got tense shoulders or neck and see if he'll rub them for you. When he does, wriggle into it and make soft moaning noises so he knows you're really into it. The 'something in my eye' ploy – pretend to have something in your eye so that he has to get right up close to you and have a look. If he still doesn't get the message, kiss him full on the lips. That tends to do the trick.

7. If you make it to a 3rd date, it's extremely likely that the man will be expecting to have sex. Make sure that you are wearing your best lingerie, no control pants, and that you have shaved everything necessary. (If you are a man, at this point, please do not feel it necessary to shave your balls. It's never a close shave, and the stubble really tickles!)

8. When a man is really interested in you, he doesn't care if you don't have sex when you see him. (On those occasions, you can wear the control pants.)

9. When dating there are certain things you should always keep in stock: a selection of wine and /or other alcoholic beverages, coffee, condoms, a razor, good lingerie, and a tub of Nutella.

10. Never take anything for granted.

WHAT IS LOVE?

22/01/2015

There are questions that have been pondered by the greatest philosophers and wordsmiths of our time – 'What is love?' 'How do you put love into words?' and 'Have you ever been to Marwell Zoo?'

Robert Burns reckoned his love was like a red, red rose... but how so exactly? Was it full of thorns and speckled with aphids? The great poets and songwriters have often tried to compare love to items of sweet innocence, like roses, onions, or even butterflies. But love is such a powerful emotion, when it strikes. Not only does it have the power to turn two perfectly rational people's hearts to mush, but it also has the power to kill, maim, destroy, and turn our worlds completely upside down.

Love isn't like a butterfly. It's more like a fucking tsunami.

My friend Imogen recently texted me with news of her love life. She said 'There's no bloody hope for me now, I'm afraid, I'm completely smitten.'   But why was she afraid? Isn't love supposed to be a 'many splendored thing'?

She was afraid because she knows only too well the way that love messes us up. Once you fall for that other person, you are completely at their mercy. They suddenly have the power to hurt you and to make you attend Coldplay concerts, completely against your wishes. And never mind what you thought you wanted, or what deep opinions you held....those things become as pliable as plasticine once you're in love. If, as a singleton, you hated Chris Martin, you will now, very slowly, almost imperceptively, start to love and admire him and want to bear his children (even if you are a bloke.)

Have you ever heard your married friends saying 'We think this...' or 'We think that...' Be prepared, because YOU too, are about to become a WE. (And you said you'd never sink so low.)

'WE want to go to Marwell Zoo.' 'WE're off to Egypt to see the pyramids and stuff!' 'WE love mascarpone.'

In the blink of an eye your individuality is cast to the wind, but you don't seem to mind too much, because you're just so caught up with being in a couple. You feel like you've just conquered the Countdown Conundrum, you've been set loose from the Stigma of Singledom, and you have finally wandered in to the world of 'We'.

'But Sharon...' I hear you say, 'How do you know when lust and romance have turned into love?' (Why are you asking me? Like I'm supposed to know...)

When I was younger, it was easy. I just knew. At least I thought I did. Love was so much easier in my twenties – it didn't really matter too much who I loved, just that I loved someone. When I first started dating Jack after I broke off my engagement, I was in no doubt, fairly early on, that I was in love. Total, all-encompassing, mad, crazy love. I hated being without him, I wanted to spend every minute of every day with him, listening to what he had to say, him making me laugh, and even listening to his collection of humorous Northern music. That's how dedicated I was.

But now I'm in my forties, and have gained my independence, and a better idea of who I am and what I want, how will I tell when I'm in love? Will I eventually get that same feeling of not wanting to be without that other person for a moment? Or is it different now that I'm older?

So, with this issue in mind, I did the first thing that everyone does when they have a burning question, or have found some strange unrecognisable growth somewhere about their person ...I Googled it.

I found myself staring at a checklist...

They are the best part of your day.
They are the first person you think about.
You prioritise their needs above your own.
You'd do anything for them.
You are not afraid to express your feelings publicly to them.
You even love their flaws.
You're considering them long-term.
They make you a better person.
You value their opinions.
You love them unconditionally.
They are your best friend.
You'd watch a Coldplay concert with them.

OK I added that last one in myself. But you get the point.

So, do I agree with that list? Yes I do. I'd have a couple more additions for the list though...

You admire and respect them.
They make you laugh.

I recently started dating someone lovely that I really like and admire, and who actually likes and admires me and treats me with respect.

I feel that I may very well fall in love with him, but I'm wondering when I will know for sure. And will he fall in love with me in return? We will have to wait and see what happens. I don't think he's a big Coldplay fan though, so I'm pretty safe there.

I LOVE YOU MORE THAN BISCUITS

Has your partner ever asked you to give up something for them? You know, like smoking, or beer, or eating Custard Creams in bed at night? How did you feel about it? Did you resolutely refuse to change, or did you jump at the chance to make your loved one happy at any cost?

Just how much are we prepared to give up for love, for fear of losing our partner? You might say you'll give up meat if you're dating a vegetarian, or wheat if you're dating a coeliac, or even butterfly jigsaws if you're dating me.   But what if your partner expects you to give up one of your favourite things? Would you do it?

I've just asked Imogen this question, and she says that she's never been asked to give up anything, and that your partner should just love you the way that you are. And she's quite right. If your partner professes to love you unconditionally, why would they ask you to give up something you love to please them?

There's only one thing I really believe should be given up for the one you love, and that's smoking (or any similarly unhealthy habit.) It can kill you and harm others around you.   But what about something as innocent as playing your favourite sport, or watching Downton Abbey? Must one be forced to give those up for one's partner as well?

So what are the types of thing that a man might ask a woman to give up?

Funnily enough, going from my experience, I can't really think of anything that a man has ever asked a woman to give up. I mean apart from me and the guys who've told me I should be a smaller size in order to have the pleasure of their fair (and obviously perfect) company.

I do know of women who give up their brains and actually dumb down to get a relationship, which seems pretty stupid to me. Surely if a guy likes you, he should like you for your intelligence too.

Women, it seems, can be slightly harder to please than men...

So, what might a woman ask a man to give up?

- Playing basketball / football
- Watching basketball / football
- Playing Call of Duty / Minecraft
- Watching 'Games of Thrones' / porn
- Wearing that terrible Argyle sweater / beanie hat
- Going to the pub
- Making cheesecakes
- Seeing other female friends

Seeing your female friends, once you're in a relationship, can be a tricky one to handle, especially if your girlfriend is of a jealous nature. There are several ways to deal with it – you either give up seeing your female friends completely, see your female friends only with your girlfriend present, or continue seeing your female friends and try to convince your girlfriend that you have no romantic interest in them. (Who are we kidding?)

Loving someone doesn't mean giving up everything for them. If there are compromises to be made, they should be made on both sides, and one partner shouldn't be left feeling that they've had to make all the sacrifices to accommodate the relationship.

I spent years of my life being a bit overweight, having guys tell me that they'd like me if only I was skinny, and I often felt under pressure to go on a huge diet and lose all the extra pounds. But something was subconsciously holding me back...the thought that actually I didn't want to go out with a guy who was shallow enough to think like that. I kept hold of those extra pounds in the hope that I would find somebody that actually liked me for me.

I'll give up the biscuits when I'm good and ready, after all they won't kill me. Or will they?

Death by biscuits
I've quite often pondered
When I'm on my own
How difficult it would be to
Get struck down by a Bourbon.
The sheer size of a Wagon Wheel's
Enough to crush one's head
But how many other biscuits
Could render a person dead?
A well-placed Chocolate Finger
Could make a grown man scream
But what about the huge dead-count
Of the Custard Cream?
A more innocent and tasty snack
You couldn't hope to find
But dunk it in your cup of tea
You may end up half blind.
And what about the cookie

Oh, chocolate spotted treat
Or the plain Digestive
That's full of whole-grain wheat?
A Rich Tea or a Ginger Nut
May sound like just a joke
But you'll not be laughing
When their crumbles make you choke.
The Jaffa-cake's the safest bet
Cos no-one ever died
Of count of misadventure
With that tangy orange side.
So just remember when you are
A dunkin' in your drink
The chance of Hobnob homicide's
More likely than you think!

WHAT DO WOMEN WANT?

I suppose, if you're a man, it can sometimes be a little confusing trying to understand what goes on in a woman's head - what they're thinking, how they're feeling, whether they're about to throw something at your head for no apparent reason...

But casting aside the monthly hormonal horrors for one moment, I'm going to try to unravel a little of the mystique here. For the most part, when it comes to men, women don't really know what they want until they're presented with it, and that I say from personal experience.

A woman can have a relationship checklist as long as your arm, but when push comes to shove they can find themselves falling for someone who doesn't necessarily fit their usual criteria.

Before writing this, I asked a few women for an idea of some of the items on their checklists. They included:

Good sense of humour
Nice smile / nice teeth
Driving ability
Lack of hairy back
No earrings
No beards

No beige underpants
No fussy eaters
Not already married

But what if you get most of those things, but he has a hairy back or he has a pair of beige underpants? Are we really going to be so shallow as to make those deal-breakers?

Some women have overly long checklists that seem to rule out anyone but some romantic hero from a Disney animated movie... It's no wonder that they cannot find their perfect man – he doesn't exist.

Manly – must be able to fix plumbing, put up shelves and look good on horseback
Handsome – must look like George Clooney
Honest – must always tell the truth, apart from when my bum really does look big in this
Intelligent – Mensa candidate
Interesting – must love current affairs, and not be interested in butterflies or jigsaws
Confident – must be socially self-assured in all situations
Financially stable – own car, own house, good management job
Kind – must support charities, love animals and be kind to waiters
Chivalrous – must behave as a gentleman at all times

Fit – must go to the gym twice a week, and run the London Marathon
Ambitious – must want to get to the top of his game, and I don't mean on the PS4
Tall – between 6'0" and 6'2" is a must
Creative – must like writing, reading and painting.
Brown eyes

But ladies, you cannot have it all!

So let's drop the checklist and go back to the essentials. Never mind what we say we want, what do women actually need?

Understanding
I know what you men are thinking – how can I understand the inconceivable, the irrational, or the illogical? Why does she change her mind every 5 minutes?
Why does it take her 2 hours to get ready to go out? But by trying to get inside your woman's head you will discover a veritable treasure trove of delights. Find out about her likes and dislikes, her childhood, her past relationships, why she enjoys doing the things she does, and what inspires her. A woman wants to feel loved, respected and admired.

She wants to know that you want to be with her for her personality and not just her looks. She wants you to share private jokes, and understand her sense of humour. She wants to know that you want to get inside her mind, and not just her knickers. Once you understand what goes on in her head, the world will be your lobster, or any other seafood of choice.

Communication

The key to any good relationship is communication, and women love it. They want to hear all about how you feel, what you want and whether or not you see a future together (in Eastbourne.) As a man, this may make you feel uncomfortable, but only if you have commitment issues, or are already married. When you're in bed with your lady and she looks into your eyes with an inquisitive look, she probably wants to silently asking you, how do you feel about me? Try not to leave it too long to tell her, because she may get bored waiting, and may dump you for being emotionally unavailable.

To Feel Valued

The woman in your life may know that she is not your first priority, but they'd like to know that they're up there in the top three, at least. Let her know she's valued, even if you can't be together all the time.

Keep her in the loop. Let her know what's going on with you and that you miss her when you can't be with her. Let her help you with something, or look after you when you have man flu. She wants to feel needed, just the same as you do.

Romance

You may not be Shakespeare or Wordsworth, but women appreciate a little romance from time to time. Most women do not naturally assume that you've done something wrong just because you buy them flowers, unless you've already told them 'I would only buy you flowers if I've done something wrong.' This is widely regarded, by women, as a bad move, and should be avoided at all cost. The buying of chocolates should also be avoided if your lady is watching her figure. Yes, it's very nice to receive a huge box of Ferrero Rocher, but be prepared for the guilt trip when she tells you she ate the lot in one go and now feels like a pregnant whale. I think that the most romantic thing you can give a woman is your time.

Faithfulness

This shouldn't be too difficult to understand. Women don't want to commit to someone who's a player, or commitment-phobic, or someone who's likely to want to sleep around with any woman that will have them.

Physical closeness

Hugging, kissing, holding hands, we love all that. The more tactile you are with us, the more we'll get the feeling that we are loved and cared for.

So What Do Men Want?

Let's look at this issue from the woman's perspective. We also have no idea what you men want either! When posed this question, one of my male cousins answered 'Big tits. No teeth.' I think that says it all.

KEEP CALM...AND THEN ROLL YOUR EYES

Picture the scene... (or don't, if you're of a nervous disposition)... You're lying in bed / on the sofa / on the backseat of a car / on your kitchen floor (delete as per preference) with your new partner – and when I say new, I don't mean this is your first date, I mean it's like your 3rd or 4th, at least, and you've already pretty much decided that he's a great catch and you'd like to have a relationship with him. You've just ended up in bed (or wherever) for the first time – and he suddenly says or does something which takes you completely by surprise, and I'm not talking about the tongue in the ear thing.

There you were, thinking that this was it, that he was the one, when he's just revealed that he: has a foot fetish / likes to dress up as Nigella Lawson / wants you to put him in a nappy and bottle-feed him.

What do you do when this happens? What's the correct etiquette for such an occasion? If you're British, the etiquette is to smile sweetly and nod in understanding, while simultaneously contemplating how best to get him out of your bed / house / car as quickly as possible.

My friend Scarlet found herself in a similar situation not so long ago. Her first date with a very handsome, city-working, Ralph Fiennes look-a-like was going very well, when he decided to mention that he was into 'watersports' and he wasn't talking about jet-skiing or scuba diving or that kind of dangerous extreme fishing that Jeremy whats-his-name does. He meant he liked women to pee on him. Scarlet just got up and left, which I think is a pretty brave move. I think many of us, myself included, would have sat there stunned, for a moment, and then politely changed the subject...
'So, have you ever been to Marwell Zoo?'
I've so far been lucky enough to not have anything too disturbing thrust at me, in a bedroom sense, from anyone I've actually been on a date (or in bed) with (accepting appendages of either massive or teeny proportions, or those with a strange bend in them) so maybe these real-life, in-person scenarios are rare. I think, men mostly tend to mention their strange perversions by text, sometime between the 1st and 2nd date.

If you spend long enough on online dating sites, you're bound to come across all manner of perversions and strange requests. If you're like me, you'll find ways of not only dealing with the perverts and sex pests, but also amusing yourself in the process, with some quippy one-liners.

'What are you wearing?'
'Scuba gear.'

'Where are your hands?'
'On a biscuit.'

'What's your cup size?'
'Espresso.'

'What would you do if you were locked in a room with me?'
'I'd claw my way out with my bare hands.'

'What if I was in bed with you right now?'
'My dog would bite your balls off.'

'How can I make you moan in bed?'
'Tell me that you haven't put the bins out.'

'What's your favourite position?'
'In front of the fridge, with the door open.'

'What's your fantasy?'
'To win the lottery, travel around the world, get my book published and stop lowering my standards enough to chat to knobheads like you.'

You can have all manner of fun at their expense. Try it sometime, when you've got a few hours spare of a Saturday evening, and you find yourself in front of a computer with nothing to Google, no online shopping to do, and no one of any interest to poke on Facebook. Log onto one of the chat sites, input some appallingly suggestive alias like 'MissBigBaps' and watch the messages roll in. Or you could opt to switch on the telly and watch 'Take Me Out,'instead. To be honest I can't decide which is less appealing, but I can guarantee that chatting to a few cybersex enthusiasts online will give you far more insight into humanity than watching some lame excuse for 'Blind Date' - where 30 single women dumb themselves down to a state of near unconsciousness in a battle to win the heart of some poor bastard and a holiday to some place that sounds like a bad fried chicken restaurant. I think somebody needs to write that in the billings.

Wasn't telly so much better in the old days, when there were only 4 channels?

Anyway, when it comes to dating shows, what the public really want is real life, not this scripted, formatted nonsense. If you really want to see what dating is like in the real world, get out there and experience it for yourself. I promise you, it will open your eyes!

___

DON'T FORGET YOUR TOOTHBRUSH

23/02/15

As previously stated, it's been a long time since I had a long-term relationship, and I suddenly find myself in a situation I haven't experienced for many, many years. I've now been dating someone for over a month. How did that happen?

And when he asked me, the other night, if he could leave a toothbrush in my bathroom, I nearly passed-out in delight.

But apart from being happy, I am also scared shitless. Why am I scared? Well, I would have thought that after reading this book, you'd have been able to answer that question yourselves. I am scared because I have the world's worse luck with relationships and dating.

For most people, who aren't me, relationships probably run fairly smoothly. You meet someone, you fall in love, you move in together, you get married, you have kids, the sex stops, you regret having the kids, the kids

Eventually move out, but now you're too tired to care about having sex, and you just grow old together and delight in watching 'Pointless' with the volume turned up so loud that you can't hear each other speak. Textbook.

My relationships have always run one of two ways:

1. I meet someone, I fall in love, they run away.
2. I meet someone, I put up with his nonsense for a while, before coming to my senses and getting out.

I will admit to having made some bad choices in my past relationships, but now that I'm older, I hope that I have enough life experience to make the right ones. Mistakes are made to be learnt from, and I am constantly learning from mine.

I am finally dating someone who is a proper grown-up. How do I know he's a grown-up? Because on our first date, he turned up wearing suit trousers! He has his own stuff going on, and he may not be in the perfect situation and have all his 'ducks in a row' relationship wise, but I know he's a good man, he treats me well, and I care about him very much.

And so I am scared. I'm scared that something's going to come along and ruin my happiness once again. I know that this is a somewhat irrational fear, but I can't help but have the feeling that somewhere in the background, fate is just waiting to deal me a low blow once again. However, just to test the theory, I did cook him Breaded Chicken for our 2nd date, and he did actually show up, so maybe, just maybe, my bad luck is finally at an end. I can but hope.

I think our relationship, if I am allowed to call it that, is progressing well, seeing as we're still in the early days. I don't really want to go into too many details, mostly because I've told him I wouldn't be writing about him (oops!) but I did mean that I wouldn't be writing about him as a bad date. That's my story and I'm sticking with it. And no judge in the land would convict me! I hope he doesn't read this, but I know what he's like, he reads everything. He's very encouraging when it comes to my writing and he seems to like reading what I have to say. But I think I'm very lucky to have someone in my life who is so interested in what I do.

I never know when to start believing that my new relationship is serious, but I thought that the toothbrush thing was a pretty good start. Is that sad, or what?

EPILOGUE

24/02/2015

Last year turned out to be a year of ups and downs in my personal life (mostly downs) but there were also some really funny moments. I am still here and I never gave up the search for a good man to love. Even if I do die a singleton, at least I have stayed true to myself, have not settled for just any man that I didn't really love, and have not let my bad experiences get the better of me.

It's given me a great deal of pleasure, writing the blog, journals and subsequent book, and has proven quite therapeutic in some ways. Some people might comment, and certainly some of my acquaintances have already commented that 'I am too honest' but I see no harm with honesty, when it hurts no one else. I think that, too often, people try to hide from their real feelings and suffer because of it. If my honesty makes you uncomfortable, then don't read what I have to say. If you don't want to write an honest blog about your personal life, then don't you write one. But do be honest with yourself.

I wrote this book, not only to entertain, but also tell it how it really is. I hope I've demonstrated that the dating game is not for the faint-hearted. You need all your emotional strength to survive the trying-to-look-interested, the disappointments, the checklists, the put-downs, the let-downs, and the hand-me-downs. And you'll need an amazing sense of humour to laugh about it all afterwards. I believe one should always try to treat people the way that they themselves expect to be treated. Show a little respect to the person who has agreed to go on a date with you, even if they're not your cup of tea in the looks or personality department. Try to be polite – just think, maybe someday someone will treat your son or daughter the way you've just treated your date.

I'm sure some readers will be curious to know if there are any updates or follow-ups to any of the stories within this book, and there are. Some of them even have a happy ending! Of course there are still some mysteries left, but every good story has a bit of mystery, or a twist.

Firstly, my great friend, Imogen, is madly in love. She finally found a man who makes her happy and appears to care deeply for her too.

I wish her every ounce of luck with this one, but I can't help but miss our little chats about her misadventures with dating. At least I knew I wasn't alone. However great, relationships have their own problems too, and I know it's not the end of the story when you find the man you want to spend your life with.

The Freddie story was never fully resolved. I never heard anything from him, and never got any apology for his horrible behaviour. I did hear from his brother, strangely enough, who explained to me that Freddie had decided to go back to his wife because of his responsibilities to their young daughter, but I don't understand why he couldn't just say that rather than leading me on for 3 months telling me he was out of the country and making me worry so much. His brother appeared to have another agenda entirely, wanting to meet up with me for I know not what purpose, saying he just wanted to be friends. I cut off communication with him when he wouldn't tell me why exactly he wanted to be 'friends'. I've had quite enough messing around from that family and I have no intention of being friends with any of them.

After a long time without a significant other person in my life, I am currently dating a lovely man. He appreciates me for my personality, my intelligence and wit. He finds me attractive despite me being a size 16.

___

242

And even though he has his own responsibilities and complications, I know that he won't abuse my trust. Only time will tell what happens, but I know for sure, that he won't be appearing in any Bad Dates blog.

For the hopeful singletons out there, I wish you the very best of luck. You are not alone, and if you're really serious about this wanting a relationship thing, then don't give up, and don't let the hard times get you down. Persevere, and don't let your checklist get the better of you. The most important thing I can advise is to trust your instincts, and always keep your sense of humour.

It's a jungle out there, ladies and gents, so date safe, but above all, have fun, and if things get really bad you can always turn your experiences into an online comedy blog.

Acknowledgements

I'd like to thank the following people for their help and support...

Fliss Williams, who was always on the end of the phone, encouraging me, product-testing my every word, and laughing like mad at every Coldplay reference.

Sharmila Grunert, who first suggested I start sharing my experiences in a blog.

Vanessa Edwards, for her great advice and always being my rock.

Stewart Ellinson, for suggesting the book title.

To those friends, colleagues and students that read and loved the original Bad Dates blog, and gave me the encouragement to continue.

To those special people that have been my inspiration: all the bad dates I ever had, and 'Imogen', 'Scarlet', 'Dave' and Daniel.

And to Rudi Peterschinnig to whom this book is dedicated, for encouraging me, and for finally breaking the curse of the Breaded Chicken.

Thank you.

A PREVIEW OF MY CURRENT NOVEL IN
PROGRESS

THORN IN MY SCYTHE

Chapter 1

It had been a particularly trying two weeks for the
Grim Reaper (Middlesex Division). First, there had
been that catastrophic multi-car pile-up on the M4,
just outside Heathrow. He'd put in a lot of overtime
on that one. When would the silly fools learn?
Always driving too close. Icy conditions. Not paying
due care and attention...and of course those
ridiculous view-obstructing pine-tree air-fresheners
that they insisted on hanging.   The guilty driver had
been too busy texting a post-Christmas break-up
message to his (now ex) girlfriend and hadn't seen
the badger amble out from the hard shoulder until it
was too late. He'd swerved to avoid it, crashing side-
on into a refrigerated meat lorry, the latter ending
up on its side across both carriageways, with its
contents spilled all over the motorway.

The resulting pile-up had caused the deaths of 23 people – at least, the Reaper had made a head-count of 23 – but what with the confusion over which meat belonged with whom and whether it was human or bovine, who knew? The Reaper only hoped that he hadn't mistakenly admitted any human-cow hybrids into the Great Beyond.

One of the victims, a Yorkshireman, who had been driving a Volvo estate, had made a terrible fuss about it all, despite the fact his soul was only tethered by a wispy thread, for which The Reaper would soon be putting his scythe to good use.

"Barrington Lancelot Bottomly?" The Reaper had asked.

"Er...that's me...yes" replied the driver timidly, as he propped himself up and stared into the apparition's dark eyes. "But you can call me Barry... if you like." Mind you, Barry thought, a man that tall could call him whatever he damned well liked, quite frankly.

"Very well." The Reaper cleared his throat. "...Barry," he said uncomfortably, for he wasn't used to informalities, "I shall take you to your final destination."

"Oh right," Barry murmured, gratefully, getting to his feet. "You don't have to, you know. I can get a taxi. I was only going as far as Greenford anyway."

The Reaper looked a bit put out. He raised a tired eyebrow and sighed. Did he really have to explain this, every single time? It was getting a bit wearing now.

"No, no, no," he said curtly, shaking his head. "You're dead!" He motioned with a bony finger in the direction of Barry's lifeless body.

Barry looked down and realised his torso was several feet from where he was now standing. It was also several feet away from his legs. "And now..." The Reaper continued, "I'm taking you to your final destination."

"That isn't Greenford then?" Barry asked, shaking his head, still trying to come to terms with the situation.

"No," replied the Reaper, curtly.

"Oh..." Barry paused. "So I'm *dead* then, am I?" He repeated the word over in his head. *Dead! Dead! Dead?*

"That is correct."

"Well, this is all highly irregular," Barry fretted, glancing back at his body. He really didn't want to be dead. It was extremely inconvenient - he had far too much to do. He had reports to file, dry cleaning to collect, and a rude DVD to return to Blockbuster before 8pm. "Are you quite sure I'm dead?" he asked, hopefully. "I mean, I could just be asleep...or...or in a coma or something..."

"No. You're definitely dead," The Reaper replied. He didn't like to sugar-coat.

"Oh...right then," Barry hesitated. "So we're...er...going then, are we?"

The Reaper nodded.

"Will I be needing my coat?" Barry glimpsed over his shoulder to see if he could make out his jacket from the wreckage of his car.

"I doubt it," The Reaper grinned, wickedly. It was his idea of a joke. There wasn't much humour to be had in his profession, so he had to take the laughs where he could.

"Oh...oooh," winced Barry, in understanding. "Well, do you mind if I just call in and say hello to my Auntie Mabel? You see it's her birthday Friday week, and she'll be expecting flowers."

"Will you just shut up and come with me!" The Reaper interrupted impatiently. He was running late enough as it was – there were still another 18 souls to remove from this incident alone. All this talk was driving him insane.

"Right then," Barry said, squaring his shoulders. He took one last wistful glance behind him as he left. "Oh, look at my poor car," he cried, "Do you think that's buggered my no-claims bonus?"

The badger had survived, unscathed.

The Reaper had also been having relationship problems. The usual story – different interests, not spending enough time together, his penchant for playing chess until the early hours...the sex wasn't as good as it used to be...blah blah blah. God, she got under his skin. Not that he had much of it to get under, but if he had, she'd have been there. Like a pimple. One of those painful spots in its infancy, that you decide to squeeze too early and it makes a total mess of your face. Yeah, that was her.

They'd decided to *take a break* – her wording, not his. *Break.* She made it sound like it was only temporary, that they'd somehow manage to work this out. But he knew this was it. It was the death knell that he'd been dreading for ages. Their love was deader than the proverbial Dodo, and The Reaper was glad that he'd had nothing to do with that particular extinction. He had enough on his conscience as it was. The Dodo incident had been down to the Grim Reaper (Mauritius Division) who'd been so bored waiting for some action that he thought he'd create his own. The poor Dodo had been a sitting duck. Quite literally.

And now, just to top it all, he'd just found out he'd been made redundant. By Post-It Note. A fluorescent pink one, he was amused to note. It was attached to his P-45 form, and simply read, 'Middlesex no longer officially recognised. Sorry.' He thought it was a nice touch that they'd added the *Sorry*, but it still didn't make up for the fact that he was now out of work, with no girlfriend and no place to go. It just proved you couldn't escape officialdom – not even in death. Surely there was enough death to go around for all of them. Couldn't he just have the M4 corridor? That would be enough. Failing that, perhaps just Reading? He angrily recalled that no one had considered the *Rutland Division* to be superfluous to requirements and he was damned sure that *Rutland* no longer officially existed. He felt a strong letter coming on.

But that would have to wait. He needed to find somewhere to live. He also needed to get rid of the thumping headache that was starting to render him incapable of coherent thought.

He rested the cold grey metal of his scythe gently against his forehead, and massaged both his temples with his bony fingers. Just as he was starting to feel slightly calmer, the scythe slipped, accidentally shaving off one of his eyebrows. *Dammit*.

Chapter 2

24th January - Breaded Chicken Theory

I may have come upon an answer as to why I keep being stood-up on dates,

and I think it has something to do with breaded chicken. Every time I have cooked

breaded chicken for a date, in the past, they have either cancelled on me at the

last minute, or worse, not turned up at all. For the guy who didn't turn up to dinner

yesterday, I wasn't going to cook breaded chicken BUT I had thought about it!

Maybe it is not, as recently suspected, the Grim Reaper stalking my potential

boyfriends, killing them off before they have a chance to form a relationship

with me.

Maybe breaded chicken is the villain here. It is fowl play!

Grim Reaper (to potential date): If you turn up for your date with Grace, it will be

your last...

Breaded chicken: (silent on the matter. A sign of guilt?)

Grace finished her daily journal entry with a rough cartoon of the Grim Reaper vs a plate of breaded chicken, and today's weight – *12st 4lbs – must do better.*

No wonder she was 3 stone overweight, it was all that extra breaded chicken she'd had to finish on her own.

She was still extremely pissed off at her date, Simon, for not turning up to dinner last night – it was supposed to have been their 3rd date and she'd felt they were onto something good. There was lots of chemistry, he had a sense of humour, good taste in clothes, no sign of a hairy back...all was looking good, until last night. Nothing. No phone call. No text to say he couldn't make it. She'd waited up until 1am on the off-chance that he was just running late, but after 6 hours even Grace had to admit that it wasn't likely, and that she had been stood up, yet again. *Bastard*. This was it. She had officially had enough of men. She didn't understand what she had been doing wrong. It's not like she was clingy or the nagging kind. And she wasn't bad looking, although no model would ever been envious of her thighs. She was curvy, in a built-for-comfort-rather-than-speed sort of way, and had a great sense of humour and a generous nature, so why was she always being overlooked by the opposite sex? She was 37, for God's sake, and getting too old for this dating nonsense. She had wanted to settle down and get married, to have someone to come home to, cook meals for, and be smug-in-front-of-singletons with.

It seemed like the whole world was already married, apart from her. All her friends were now married, even the gay ones. They all either had babies or were trying for them, and whenever she phoned them for a chat, they would witter on about the sleepless nights, the nappy changing and the swollen breasts. She seemed to have nothing in common with them anymore. They would say *'You're so lucky to be free and single'*, but Grace had never felt lucky to be single. And what was the problem with having swollen breasts anyway?

Not that it mattered now. She promised herself to have nothing more to do with men; she'd been let down one too many times. There would be no more introduction agency subscriptions. No more pointless speed-dating - or *speed-friending* as she now called it - having been filed in the 'friend' zone by all the men that she had marked as potential date material. And no more internet freaks who asked for cybersex before they asked for her name.

Grace remembered her last speed-dating experience. There had been a couple of guys she had gelled with, one of them had even suggested meeting for a drink sometime, to which she had agreed. But on receiving her results after the event, it turned out that he hadn't even marked her as a 'friend'. How deceitful was that? Not that she wanted him as a friend; what was the point of coming speed-dating and marking people as 'friends'? She had enough friends; she wasn't looking for any more. She was looking for someone to love her.

Dating agency experiences had proved just as fruitless. Her last date had seemed fine on paper. His name was Neil; he liked restoring old cars, eating out and going to the cinema. He worked in IT and lived fairly locally. They'd agreed to meet in a new wine bar, a short drive from Grace's flat. He'd turned up ten minutes late, but Grace had forgiven him as soon as she'd laid eyes on his chiselled features. *Thank You, God*. He joined her at the bar and she bought him a drink, but for some reason, he seemed to have taken an instant dislike to her.

"What have you been up to today?" Grace asked, trying to break the ice.

"Sand blasting'" he said, curtly.

"Oh, on your car?"

"Yes." He seemed determined to be as short with her as possible.

"And what does the sand blasting remove?" she asked, pleasantly.

"Everything."

This was going to be a long evening. Grace drained her glass, but he didn't offer to buy her another drink. She decided to persevere.

"I saw from your profile that you speak Spanish...?"

"That's right."

"Where did you learn that?"

"Japan," he answered, sarcastically. It wasn't going well.

"What would your ideal job be if you didn't work in IT?" Grace asked, hoping to probe a bit deeper.

"I'd be a musician or a writer," he briefly brightened.

"Oh, that's great," Grace enthused; he'd finally touched upon something that they had in common. "So what instrument do you play?"

"I don't play anything."

"Oh ok. So what have you written?"

"Nothing."

Clearly, he was an idiot. It was time to bring out the big guns and put this arsehole in his place.

"I've written 2 novels," she smiled. *Grace 1, Moron 0.*

Luckily for Grace, he had made his excuses after 40 minutes and left. Obviously, he was the type that believed good looks won over charm, personality and intelligence.

Grace felt that whoever had come up with the phrase *labour of love* had probably had their fair share of dredging the depths of the single male dating pool. All this dating was hard work; it was like never getting past the interview stage for a new job – or only getting interviews for jobs you didn't really want.

She would no longer spend Valentine's Day yearning for red roses from her sweetheart, and there would be no more cooking for two.   Enough was enough. She felt like a huge weight had been lifted from her shoulders. Freedom. Now she could finally get on with her life, and stop putting it on hold for a man.

Chapter 3

The Reaper's first few days of unemployment had been strangely enjoyable and quite liberating. On Monday, after reading the 'Reaper's Digest' from cover to cover, he craved some fresh air to clear his head and decided to head out horse riding with three old mates. They took a good two-hour hack through the Buckinghamshire countryside, stopped for drinks at the Headless Horseman and reminisced about the old days.

"Remember when we wreaked havoc on the world?" The Reaper smiled.

"Yeah…good times, good times," Pestilence agreed, scratching his beard, just as War came back from the bar with the next round of Stella.

On hearing about The Reaper's unfortunate circumstances, Famine, or Fami as he affectionately called her, had been quite sympathetic to his plight and had agreed to let him stay the week on her sofa, which was a huge weight off his shoulders. The only real problem with her place was that there was never anything in the fridge.

Tuesday had been a complete write-off, nursing a hangover. All day he'd lounged around on the sofa that he now temporarily called *home*, and watched all his favourite films on DVD; *Heaven Can Wait*, *Live and Let Die*, *Final Destination I*, *II* and *III*, *Meet Joe Black*, and *Sleepless in Seattle*. He'd had to go and have a cold shower after watching the penultimate scene in *Raiders of the Lost Ark*. Those diaphanous angels of death had got him quite excited.

Wednesday had been spent in Starbucks, searching through the jobs papers. He'd already wasted an hour trying to order.   In the end he'd settled for a toffee-pecan-macchiato-frappuccino, whatever that was.   He took a long sip of it and wished he'd ordered something easier to pronounce. *Ouch! Brain freeze*.

He placed the pile of papers in front of him and started leafing through.   Nothing in The Guardian – he didn't fancy being a *Corporate Headhunter* – a little over-qualified, perhaps. *Administrator*? No, too boring. He didn't want to be stuck in an office all day long, staring at a computer screen, and besides that, he was a complete technophobe. To him, a *mouse* was something small and fluffy, to be feared, and *software* meant a nice comfy cloak.   He skimmed each page and suddenly felt drained.

What was an *Employment Engagement Adviser*? An *Information Architect*? *Head of Inclusion*? They were making it up. It was all gobbledegook. There was absolutely nothing for him. What was he qualified for? What had all those years of Reaping prepared him for? Certainly not for *Head of Inclusion*, that much he was sure of.

His office had provided him with a more-than-satisfactory redundancy pay-off, excellent references, and all the paperwork he needed to start a new life among the mere mortals. But they hadn't prepared him for this... Total Hopelessness.

He had been issued with a new ID, passport, driving licence, birth certificate, Tesco Clubcard... He glanced at his new passport – terrible photo – he looked like death. And his new name? Graham Reaper. *Great*. He had to go through the rest of his life being called Graham. Could things get any worse? He reasoned that it probably could – he could have been an *Information Architect*. But for the moment he would have to swallow his pride and sign on, jobless.

Having had enough of trying to squeeze his six-foot-five frame onto Fami's five-foot sofa, he decided it was time to find a place of his own to rent. A studio apartment would do. Just one room was all he really needed. He didn't have a lot of stuff – there was his scythe, of course, plus a couple of cloaks, an old vinyl of Dance Macabre by Saint-Saëns, and his Coldplay CDs. He packed the smaller belongings into a cardboard box, wished Fami all the best and set off on his way.

Being a Reaper, albeit an ex one, had its advantages. He checked-in with his ex employer's office, leafed through his old records, and was pleased to note that Malcolm Wilson, a middle-aged bachelor, who he had recently taken over to the other side, had left a one bedroom flat in Pinner which fitted the bill perfectly. He contacted the relatives, who were more than happy to have someone renting the place, which they were having trouble trying to sell. Something about the circumstance of the death were putting people off buying it. Graham didn't really worry that Mr Wilson had died wearing a pair of silk stockings, with a bin bag over his head and an orange in his mouth. At least the victim had had the decency to look embarrassed about it. The Reaper chuckled to himself remembering the last words he'd heard Malcolm say.

"Oh God, oh God, oh God! Not now!" He'd cried. "Please can you just let me take the stockings off? Please?" The Reaper had denied the request.

Made in the USA
Charleston, SC
13 March 2015